EVERYTHING YOU NEVER WANTED TO KNOW ABOUT YOUR NONPROFIT CORPORATION

A Handbook For Unaware Volunteers

By

Ms. Cellaneous

The Unknown Attorney

Bellissima Publishing, LLC

Jamul, California

This book contains general information and is the opinion of only one person. Laws vary from state to state. For specific advice on any area of the law, you should consult your own attorney.

Copyright © 2005 by Bellissima Publishing

All rights reserved. No part of this book may be reproduced or transmitted in any means whether, mechanical, electronic or photocopying or recording, or any information storage and retrieval system without express, written permission from the publisher.

Published by Bellissima Publishing, LLC, Jamul, California
www.bellissimapublishing.com

Printed in the United States of America

ISBN 0-9768417-0-3
First Edition

To my husband, who is also unknown and likes it that way!

Table of Contents

Chapter One
Look Before You Leap! (Or Playing Leap Frog Can Get You Into Trouble!)..1

Chapter Two
Check Out the Employees of the Nonprofit Corporation....................5

Chapter Three
The Child Molester...9

Chapter Four
Now What?..15

Chapter Five
The Great Takeover..21

Chapter Six
So What Did the Bad Guys Get? What Did They Do To Get What They Got?...27

Chapter Seven
Always Do the Right Thing and Please Sell your Candy Bars, As Well as Other Related And Miscellaneous Matters 31

Chapter Eight
Kids Get Injured Every Day, So What? 37

Chapter Nine
How Could a Thing Like This Happen?...................................,43

Chapter Ten
Be a Duck! Or Just Act Like One!...51

Chapter Eleven
Duck, Duck, Duck . . . Goose! 57

Chapter Twelve
We Did the Only Thing We Could Do! ……………………………..63

Chapter Thirteen
Why Didn't We Just Give Them the Corporation? ………………75

Chapter Fourteen
The Good, The Bad and The Ugly …………………………………...83

Chapter Fifteen
The Articles of Incorporation …………………………………….....87

Chapter Sixteen
Writing Your Bylaws or Changing Them to Protect Your Corporation…95

Chapter Seventeen
Make Your Coach Contracts Stand For Something…………………111

Chapter Eighteen
The Immigration Reform and Control Act, Form I-9 ……………117

Chapter Nineteen
The letter of Termination   …………………………………………..123

Chapter Twenty
Letters of Tax Exempt Status ……………………………………129

Chapter Twenty-One
Your Application for Membership……………………………………..135

Chapter Twenty-Two
They Want the Rules, So Give Them the Rules, Or Just Let them Eat Cake! ………………………………………………………………..141

Chapter Twenty-Three
Insurance and Medical Waivers………………………………………..155

Chapter Twenty-Four
The Honor Code……………………………………………………..185

Chapter Twenty-Five
The Team Commitment Form ……………………………..……...171

Chapter Twenty-Six
It Can't All Be Bad……………………………………………………181

Chapter Twenty-Seven
So What Else Do You Have To Do?..187

Chapter Twenty-Eight
The Devil Made Me Do It!..193

Chapter Twenty-Nine
Exactly What Does the Law and the IRS Say?.....................................197

Chapter Thirty
Keeping the Alligators Out of the Swamp……………………………. .201

Chapter Thirty-One
The Law is the Law, And Sorry Folks, But What I Am Saying Is true!..205

Forward……………………v

About The Author…………………vi

FORWARD

The Unknown Lawyer has been practicing law in the State of California for over twenty years. What you are about to read is true. No names have been used to protect the innocent. In case you are wondering as you read this handbook, the innocent are herein referred to as the "good guys". The good guys have given the unknown lawyer explicit permission to write this book and to tell their story. As you read through the jungle that is their story, please be aware that this could happen to you. This handbook is written to protect the children of the future that they may not be used, abused or have what is precious stolen from them.

Our children are our future, and without our future we are lost. We must all serve as example of what is good, right and just.

Up in the sky! Is it bird? Is it a plane? No. It's the Unknown Attorney, fighting a battle for truth, justice and the American way!

This handbook is intended to reveal in a frank and discerning matter exactly what can happen and did happen to one nonprofit organization and seeks to prevent its occurrence in the future. It is a step by step guide with reference as to how to form and protect you child's sport's team's nonprofit corporation booster club. If this handbook helps one person see the truth and prevents what happened to us from ever happening again, then everything we all went through will be worth it.

I am the Unknown Attorney.. My identity is confidential. My heart is most sincere. My name shall forever remain, Ms Cellaneous.

About The Author

The unknown attorney has been practicing law for over twenty years in the State of California. She has been widely published in the area of business law and if you knew the identity of the Unknown attorney you could find her work in such past publications as *Sound and Video Contractor Magazine*, *Business Radio Magazine*, and *Broadcast Engineering Magazine*. The unknown attorney was an educator prior to entering the field of law, and as an educator was published in *The Kindergartner*, and *Instructor Magazine*. She has also been published in *Humpty Dumpty Magazine*. The Unknown Attorney loves children and is devoted to them. It is for this reason, and for this reason alone, she embarked upon this work Watch for additional works of the Unknown Attorney coming to your bookstore soon, as the Unknown attorney fights for truth, justice and the American way!

EVERYTHING YOU NEVER WANTED TO KNOW ABOUT YOUR NONPROFIT CORPORATION

A Handbook For Unaware Volunteers

Everything You Never Wanted To Know About Your Nonprofit Corporation

Chapter One

Look Before You Leap! (Or Playing Leap Frog Can Get You Into Trouble!)

You have never volunteered for anything in your life, but now you feel inexplicably drawn to little Sally's swim team booster club or little Johnny's soccer team or Little League parent volunteer group. You're just helping the children, right? There's nothing wrong with helping the children. Right? Wrong! There can be many legal and emotional pitfalls for you ahead if you are not careful, and some even if you are careful. What can you do about it? Don't run across that soccer field with abandon or jump into the deep end of the volunteer pool without being informed, because somewhere between. handing out hotdogs at the snack bar or serving as timer at the end of a swimming pool lane, you may be asked to serve on the board of directors of that certain nonprofit corporation that supports your child's team, and before you agree to any of it, make sure you know your rights and responsibilities in relation to that nice little team you have agreed so selflessly to help and support.. Be ready to pick up the bat and make a home run hit.

Ascertain if your nonprofit corporation is in good standing with the state in which it is incorporated.

As unbelievable as it sounds, many nonprofit corporations, unbeknownst to its individual members, are not in good standing with the state in which the corporation is allegedly incorporated; and this alone can cause a myriad of problems. In California, for example, a suspended corporation has lost all legal rights and can only legally amend the articles of incorporation, file a statement of information (listing its corporate offices and agent for service of process), and/or change its name. If the suspended corporation enters into any contracts while in suspension these contracts are voidable at the option of the opposite party to the contract. If the corporation is sued, it cannot appear in court because it has no legal standing. Statutes of Limitations are not tolled during the period of suspension, and the corporation will have a difficult time doing any business outside the state of California because of full faith and credit laws of other states. If the suspended corporation acts as though it is a valid corporation in good standing, it may be found liable for intentional misrepresentation, or even criminal fraud, depending on the particular facts and circumstances of the situation, and without the protection of the corporate entity, there is no corporate veil, and the so-called board of directors of the corporation may be held individually liable for not only the debts of the corporation, but the acts of individuals hired by the suspended corporation as the corporation is legally, and therefore factually, nonexistent..

How do you find out if your corporation is in good standing? The answer to this is quite simple. Each state keeps a record of its corporations, and this record will show the status of the corporations within the state. You can check on line, or call the department of corporations or the secretary of state of the state and simply find out the status. First you find out in what state the nonprofit corporation you are investigating has been incorporated, and then you go on line using your internet search engine or call the state and simply ask them how you find out what you need to know. Never be afraid to ask about anything. The only stupid question is the question you were either afraid to ask, too stupid to ask, or forgot to ask. Question everything, and if you can't get an answer run as fast as you can. A judge once told my opposition in court that if it smelled like a fish, then it probably was a fish, so if you can't get the answers for which you are looking, then you have more than likely netted a fish, and if you accept a position on a board of directors of any nonprofit corporation, no matter what it is, even a church, without checking out the organization thoroughly, then you could clearly find yourself in trouble later.

What happens if you discover Sally's swim team booster club is not a corporation in good standing with the state in which it is incorporated and/or is in suspension? Find out why and then try to fix the problem, or move Sally to another team. Why do this? Because if the booster club owns or manages the team, your team's insurance may be in jeopardy. Why would the team's insurance be in jeopardy? It would be in jeopardy because insurance is a contract, and when a corporation is in suspension, then its contracts entered into while in suspension are voidable by a party other than the suspended corporation, and more specifically, the corporation itself does not have any legal standing to go to court to enforce anything. If the club purchased the insurance, and the club no longer legally exists, the insurance company now has grounds for not honoring claims, and if little Sally breaks an arm or a leg running on the pool deck or across a soccer field there may be no insurance for board of directors' protection, making the board of directors individually liable.

Rest assured that the insurance company will not honor any claims it does not have to honor, and if the corporation has no legal standing, as in California, then the suspended corporation cannot go to court to enforce the terms of the insurance policy, leaving the board of directors without any legal teeth. Remember that the fewer claims your organization's insurance company is forced to honor, the higher will be its profits. Your organization's insurance company is never your friend no matter how many pocket calendars they send to you for Christmas!

If it sounds scary, that's because it is scary, so step one is to look before you leap and check to see if the organization you have grown to know and to love has an actual and valid nonprofit status.

Chapter Two

Check Out the Employees of the Nonprofit Corporation

What you think you see, may not be what you are getting, so check out the employees of the nonprofit corporation before you get on board. Ask to see the actual proof the employees are not only properly credentialed, but watch and observe how the employees of the most wonderful swim team in the world act and interact with the children, and then check and double check and don't believe anything you are told and only half of what you see. People forge these things, so go straight to the governing body of the sport and affirm even what you have seen with your own eyes.

I was pro bono counsel for a swim team booster club, for example, that had a coach who was coaching for several years without a USA coach's certification card. This not only voided all swim team insurance coverage for the swim team, but it also voided all the insurance for everyone at any swim meet or event while this so-called coach stood on the deck, and resulted in one or more swim meets actually being decertified. Also, don't believe that even if you find out something like this that you will be either believed, or you will be able to get other parents to actually take this coach off the pool deck or soccer field for a minute, because parent/coach/kid loyalties seem to run inexplicably deep and are filled with all sorts of irrational emotions, and the coach who has been able to do this knows just how to play this to his benefit. What should you do? If no one will listen to you, then run as fast as you can away from that team no matter how much little Sally pleads with you to stay. Do not accept a position on that board of directors if you can't change this or at least get that coach off the deck until he or she is properly licensed by the sport's governing body.

Again, how do you find out the status of a coach's credentials? As stated above, simply call the governing body of the sport and just ask. If you don't know who the governing body is or where it is, ask until you find out. You need to do this for yourself. You need to police those who are in charge of your child to make sure they have proper credentials. Do not expect the governing body of the sport to police this for you. In fact, USA Swimming requires its swim clubs to make sure its coaches are properly credentialed and completely relieves the local swimming committees from this responsibility, even though the local swimming committees have ready access and are endangering swimmers by voiding insurance when these individuals stand on deck at a sanctioned swim meet with other teams totally unaware of and not responsible for the credentialing of these coaches, and even though under the USA Swimming Insurance, insurance for all swimmers on deck is voided. It doesn't matter what you think or expect will be done for your child. Expect nothing from anyone, and even expect to be viewed with suspect when you ask these questions. Some people may even get angry with you, and this is the only thing you can expect, especially if you uncover a problem.

Now if you are a coach owned swim team and your booster club is ancillary to the team owned by the coach and he is not hired by you, who is responsible to make sure the coach is properly credentialed when he goes on a pool deck at either a swim meet or to coach a practice? Well, it isn't USA Swimming, and it isn't the local swimming committee, it is the team, and if the team is owned by the coach, then that would logically be the coach which means if his credentials lapse and he is on deck and insurance is voided he may be held liable if anything bad happens on that deck, whether or not it was his fault because he caused all the insurance to be voided. In the least he will be sued, but chances are he doesn't have any money; and if he is a child molester volunteer, then he is probably also judgment proof. Who knows how soccer or little league or any other sport works. If you are with any other sport, you should probably find out.

So if your swim coach is employed by your nonprofit organization and has no coach's card, and the result is your insurance is claimed void, where then would the liability lie? You got it! Liability would lie with the employing corporation, and if that corporation is suspended, then the liability could flow to the individual board members. Think this could never happen? Think again. It happened to that swim team club I represented pro bono, no coach's card, no corporate entity as it was suspended! Luckily, there was no resulting incident creating liability. Do not take anything for granted. Check on those coaching credentials, even if the coach is your own brother! Even if the coach is like a family member! Even if the coach is your best friend! Trust no one. You are doing this for little Sally, after all, and little Sally deserves nothing but the best!

   Check. Question. Check again. Leave no stone unturned. My little Sally told me she didn't think her coach had a coaching card, and I didn't believe her. She said when she looked at his coaches card it had another name on it, and when she asked him where his card was, he told her it was in the bottom of his briefcase leading her to the conclusion her coach had no coach's card. Did I believe her? The answer is no. I thought this coach was absolutely wonderful because he told me everything I wanted to hear about my own child. Do not be fooled by flattery. Your child is probably not Olympic bound, and extra attention to your child may even be a red flag for you to stop and think about what you have seen and observed up until this time. Take off the rosy glasses and take a really good look. Question everything. The most stupid of all questions is the question you ask no one, not even yourself. Remember this is all about little Sally, not about you, no matter how much your chest fills with pride as little Sally swims across that swimming pool or makes that soccer goal. Don't be a fool with blinders. Open your eyes before you get dangerously blind sighted. It may hurt, but you will get over it.

Chapter Three

The Child Molester

When parents place a child on any sports team, they do not expect their child will be molested. They expect that whoever hired those in charge of their children has run a thorough background check and that their child is safe. They have every reasonable right to expect this under the law. This is why before you accept a position on any nonprofit corporation board you need to ask if the coaches this board has hired have run a background check on each and every coach hired. Fingerprinting should be standard for optimal safety. Do not accept the word of anyone. If you are able to, go on line on the internet and run an outstanding warrant search through your local sheriff or police department's warrant site. Do not expect the local sports governing body to have done any of this for you. Remember that child molesters go where the children are; and good, competent coaching is a full time job, so if someone is doing this for free, be suspicious of their intent. Be suspicious of the intentions of anyone who is not paid as an employee of the organization and who is volunteering for the organization when they have no children involved in the sport, or who hang around and keep volunteering after their minor children have left the sport all together. There is no free lunch. These so-called volunteers more than likely have some sort of interest in hanging around, either monetary or otherwise; and while you may come across the occasional altruistic individual, put no faith in your own instincts to believe the best of anyone like this at any time. Ask if fingerprint checks and background investigations have been run on employees before you step up to the plate.

Shortly after one particular coach was fired from our age group swim team (for unrelated reasons), the rumor went around at a swim meet that this individual had an inappropriate sexual relationship with a minor girl he had been coaching at the high school where he coached and for that reason was asked to vacate his position and was thereafter terminated. A call to the police department and to the high school principal confirmed this fact as presumed true, although the mother of the child opted not to press charges after the initial filing of the complaint. It took only two phone calls to substantiate this, and anyone could have done exactly what I did. I was told this coach should have never been granted high school clearance to coach by the high school principal in charge of the program because there was a pattern of behavior discoverable by contacting those for whom this coach had previously worked. To top it off, this coach was a volunteer coach through the high school and was not being paid. This is why I say to be suspicious of anyone who is volunteering to be around children without compensation or a child involved in the sport giving them a reason to be there.

Statutory rape does not allow a minor to consent to a sexual act. Statutory rape occurs when an adult over the age of consent in the particular state has a sexual relationship another individual who is under the age of consent in that state. Australia makes coaches at major swim meets sign an involved declaration under penalty of perjury that they have not engaged in any such acts and the declaration goes so far as to even describe exactly what they mean by this. Perhaps your club should adopt a similar document to protect the organization as well as its board of directors. It couldn't hurt! It might help. Legally, it may help your organization and/or the board of directors. (If the organization is in suspension and there is therefore no protective corporate veil over the board of directors, the board of directors will need all the legal protection they can get.)

Believe it or not, the child molester referred to above continues to this day to coach young girls through USA Swimming and parents who have now hired him refuse to believe or even investigate whether the rumors are true, when all they need to do is make two simple phone calls. When a policeman and a school principal tells you a coach has no business being around young girls, you tend to listen, so if you don't make the call either you don't want to know the truth, or you are contributorily negligent in allowing the molestation of your own child, if not legally, then morally, not to mention your legal, moral and ethical obligations to other children.

Never presume the local sports committee will help you with this problem, or even that the national governing board will listen to you and do anything about this individual. If you are on a board of directors and you have not done a proper investigation of your employees, your organization is more than likely going to be charged with some sort of negligence should a molestation occur, and even if you try to tell the local sports governing body about this, you may also expect a degree of passing the buck and a shifting of the onus of responsibility back to you. They may even become defensive towards you for reporting the alleged problem. What they don't realize is once they are aware of the situation, the problem shifts to them to do something about it and to act with prudence because knowing of the alleged problem, not investigating it, and then letting this individual continue to have authority and control over children places additional children in harm's way, and it is all too foreseeable the problem will occur again. In fact, it is so foreseeable, it is a problem waiting to happen. Your organization should simply fire the bastard!

One should always do the right thing, but please do not expect that doing the right thing will be an easy task. Unfortunately, most people would rather bury their heads in the sand than open their eyes wide and see and then do the right thing. An ounce of prevention is worth a pound of cure.

What should good coaches not do?

If you see a coach open his long swim parka wide and offer to let a young girl inside to hug her, be suspicious unless the girl is his sister. If you see a pre-teen girl sting on a coach's lap or invited by the coach to sit on his lap, especially when she is wearing nothing but a swim suit, be suspicious. If your child is singled out and told he or she is the coach's favorite, be suspicious. If your child receives special gifts from the coach that no one else receives, be suspicious. If the coach invites your child to go alone with him to the movies or anywhere else alone, or if you hear this is happening to another child, be suspicious. I have seen all of this happen right in front of my own face. Child molesters call this grooming. It is very scary. If you are involved in an organization and are on its board of directors, and if you have any knowledge of any kind that a coach is acting in appropriately and you do nothing to curb it, stop it or investigate it, your organization may end up being found negligent in a court of law should a child be molested, because as the employers of these individuals your organization owes a certain duty of care to those children in the care of those whom your organization has hired. Also, if the organization is in a suspended status and has no valid and legal nonprofit corporate identity, the liability would flow to the board of directors because there would be no protective corporate veil.

Therefore, prior to leaping into that board of directors position, make certain there us a valid corporate entity that is not in suspension, that the coaches all have proper coaching credentials, and that no coach hired or under your control has any adverse history of any kind.

Think this could never happen in your organization? Think again. And please do not expect anyone to readily believe you about anything, or even expect that they will check the facts on their own, even if you tell them who to call and hand them the phone numbers... I can almost guarantee there will be people who do not believe you. . . even if you are an attorney. I can guarantee it because it happened to me.

Remember, you are doing this for the children and for no one else but the children. This is not a popularity contest, and if you expect it to be one, then just do not volunteer because chances are you will be very disappointed in the outcome. You may not be successful in getting the child molester away from children, but you can remove your child from the child molester, and this is a start. Until a parent is willing to file charges, unfortunately, thus may be all you will get. Yes, it breaks your heart, but the truth is all you can do is inform everyone in charge and in a position to do something about it, and nothing more. And yes, you have a right to do this in writing or otherwise as a communication given to one in a position to take a perceived action against a wrong, even if it turns out the information you have received is false, is protected speech and is not defamation. It is not liable or slander. Truth is also a complete defense to such a communication .as well as to anything said or written about another. Do not wait until your coach falls in love with and runs away with a minor child. At least this didn't happen to our team, but it has happened in others.

Chapter Four

Now What?

Your little Sally or little Johnny loves the organization. This is the team on which they want to play. All their friends belong to the team, and you were going to become an officer of the nonprofit booster club but discover it is in suspension. You want to save the team. You want to fix the problem. Where do you begin? Well, it is quite simple. You ask the same governmental agency who told you the organization was in suspension why it is in suspension. If you are on the board of directors of the organization you have every right to know because as soon as you were elected or appointed to the board, you became responsible for the day to day running of the business of the corporation. The state will tell you what you need to know, and then you can begin to fix it along with the other members of the board. Sometimes it is as simple as a yearly paper or document not being filed. Sometimes it is more serious, but in California, as in many other states, if you are in suspension you have no valid legal corporate identity with which to conduct business and you continue to conduct business at your own peril.

    The minute a new board of directors is elected, it should ask for an audit of the board of directors that preceded it, and if the board is one that continues from year to year, a yearly audit of the corporate books should be made. The books should be open at each board meeting for inspection. Do not trust anyone. Do not trust your treasurer with unfailing devotion to do the right thing without any checks and balances. Do not believe anything you see other than actual bank statements and canceled checks. Demand at least two signatures on every check. Why? Because when you discover your corporation is in suspension, you may also discover your treasurer has been embezzling for years, hasn't forwarded withholding from paychecks to the IRS and to the state unemployment insurance department, has lied about the amount of money in the checkbook, and has blatantly stolen from the corporation. Remember what I said about a board volunteer who has no child involved with your team, that they may have another interest in your team besides unadulterated loyalty? This is one very good place where something very bad can happen. Think it can't happen on your nice little team where you have been a member for over five years? Think that because the team is located in a nice conservative community nothing bad can happen? Think again. It can happen, will happen and does happen in team booster clubs all over the country, every single day. What you have been seeing on the outside, may not be what you will see on the inside once you give the organization a good, hard, long look. It happened to the swim team booster club I represented, so I know first hand it can, will and does happen. It happened to our booster team, and we are located in a small upper class community that rivals the fictional town of Stepford, home of the Stepford wives! We are talking about a place that is like a picture book, where kids ride bicycles down the street, surf in the Pacific Ocean and are able to walk to the beach alone without fear, and where the local police have practically nothing to do!

Yes, there is a lot you need to know, but this is why there are so many resources available to you. There are internet resources, and state specific self-help books, people to call and from whom you may ask question after question. If you don't know something, ask someone who knows. There are state and IRS publications and 800 numbers you can call that even have pre-recorded frequently asked questions and answers. No one knows everything, not even an attorney, and if you are left to put together a puzzle that has fallen on the floor, you need all the pieces of the puzzle. Don't let the dogs bury any of the pieces. If they do, then the children can't play and the game is lost.

If a coach comes to you and tells you there is no record of his employment with the IRS and social security, as happened to the board I represent, and the treasurer tells you she just forgot to file a paper, please do not take the treasurer at her word, because a very important red flag has been thrown high into the air. You need to act before the flag reaches the ground. In the instance of the board I represented no quarterly payments had been made to the IRS for approximately four full years, and missing paperwork existed even before that time. You see if the paperwork isn't filed in relation to the withholding, then the IRS has no idea how much the organization is not forwarding to the governmental agencies that it has been withholding from paychecks and allegedly held in sacred trust for the

IRS. An embezzler can get away with pocketing money for years unless or until an employee tries to collect unemployment, or simply examines the reports social security sends out in relation to employment history. An embezzler can get away with this for years if she is trusted and beloved by the corporation members because she has done so much to allegedly benefit the corporation. No one knows she is merely benefiting herself by dipping into the treasury unknown to everyone else. The best thing you can do for this person is to catch her early on, before the amount gets up to $50,000.00 (fifty thousand dollars) or more as happened in the case of the organization I represented, or maybe she would rather flee and go to jail. You should care about her enough to help her do the right thing if she is so beloved, and if she doesn't cooperate with you to fix things and make them right, tell her to go straight to jail, do not pass "Go" and do not collect two hundred dollars. In other words, file charges against her with the local police, because if you don't, you may be sorry, and sorry is not a fun "game".

If our treasurer had nothing to hide, she would have opened the books wide and explained herself when asked. She would not have gone out and hired a team of attorneys in the name of the corporation without any authorization of the corporation from which she had been terminated. And an honest attorney would simply not have assisted her in the takeover of that corporation as a means of defending her. You see once the organization was successfully taken away, then the officers who uncovered the fraud had no legal standing to file a complaint anywhere on behalf of the corporation even after the corporation was revived, so in order to protect the treasurer, the attorneys had to get rid of those who were shouting "Stop thief!" and in doing so they became accomplices in defrauding the governmental entities for whom the funds they ultimately handed to the takeover group ultimately belonged as these were funds withheld from employee paychecks and held in trust and not the assets of the corporation at all!. If I am repeating myself here, apparently I cannot say this too often because in our situation no matter how many times I said it nobody believed me, not at the local level, not even at the national sport level. Everyone was informed of everything at every step of the way and everyone was implored to do something to stop the madness. Yet the madness continued. What they all did was thereafter assist in the continued commission of a crime to defraud the employees of the corporation, the IRS, and the state government, and because I told them what they were doing, no one involved can claim ignorance. All they can claim is that they chose to believe the lies they were told instead of checking out for themselves what the truth really was. To the date of this writing I am informed and therefore believe the debts thus owed have not been paid by the takeover group and no money has been forwarded as required under law, even though I had arranged to have the funds put in trust with the state governmental entity for the benefit and claims of all creditors. Since the funds were disputed there should have been no problem with this because if there was nothing neither due and owing nor the property of the governmental entitles, then the money would have been released to the group ultimately prevailing in the dispute. If it smalls like a fish and looks like a fish, chances are it is a fish. Those who are innocent and who tell the truth have nothing to fear. Those who lie and steal must manipulate their escape any way they can.

Put quite simply, a board of directors needs to immediately demand inspection of the books, documents and other things in the possession of the treasurer, and accept no excuse. If this request is refused file a criminal complaint with the police department or local sheriff as stated above. If the treasurer has done nothing wrong, there should be no problem in cooperating. If on the other hand cooperation is refused, the treasurer has something to hide. Sound too harsh? It isn't because you cannot possibly imagine what could and might happen next, and you cannot possibly imagine what happened to the board of directors I represented who did not immediately file charges against a treasurer who embezzled from their corporation.

If you do not get immediate cooperation, go in for the kill. As I have told you, this is not about you and a popularity contest. It is about the children. Forget about your standing in the community, because if you give this person an inch she will steal a mile, and she will get help to do it.

Chapter Five

The Great Takeover

Even when you do everything right, everything can go wrong, especially when people are involved with your corporation who each have their own personal interests in your organization that have absolutely nothing to do with anything that has to do with what is right, and everything that has to do with what is self preservation and what is right for them. Do not let what happened to our corporation happen to yours. Granted, this is a worst case scenario and is actually quite unbelievable, but everything that happened to us really happened and if it happened to us it could happen to you, even if, or perhaps because of the long time apparent good standing of your organization. Also, be prepared. The truth does not always prevail and right does not necessarily defeat wrong, even if your attorney has more experience than theirs, and even if your attorney has done everything possible to preserve that which is right.

So what happened to our organization? While the organization's board of directors was busy negotiating with the local Water Polo Team to join with them and under a common umbrella of understanding to promote all aquatics sports, shortly after terminating three coaches for leaving children alone on a military base in violation of a certain memorandum of understanding between the military base, the local recreation department and the swim team booster club (this being a second violation), and after requesting certain documents from the treasurer, while it was yet not known of the violations committed under law by that treasurer, the treasurer met with the terminated coaches and several individuals new to the organization, these having been members for no more than four months, most brought to the swim team by one of the now terminated coaches (the coach who just happened to be a child molester) a conspiracy was entered into by these individuals to take over our organization. First there was a meeting called by the treasurer and a no confidence vote was taken as to all of the board of directors as well as this attorney who was serving as pro bono counsel, to remove us all from membership in the corporation. Since there was only one way to vote and because that was for no confidence, and because a quorum was not present, the vote was invalid.

In the meantime, it was discovered the corporation was in suspension by one of the board of directors of the water polo team who was investigating our team prior to opening the umbrella under which all the aquatic teams would work together. After further investigation the seriousness regarding what had been done by the treasurer was uncovered. The treasurer was asked to immediately supply books, records, documents and things to the board of directors, a board that was newly elected and had only been in office for four months. When the treasurer did not immediately comply, she was terminated from the board of directors by majority vote of the board of directors for malfeasance and as allowed under the law; and in fact as required under the law in order to immediately stop the furtherance of a crime, that being willful and knowing failure to forward money held in sacred trust, withheld from employee paychecks, as required under both state and federal law.

The terminated treasurer then hired an attorney (on behalf of and in the name of the corporation from which she was terminated and for which she had no legal authority from the corporation) who prevented the duly elected board from access to both the organization s bank account as well as to the mail of the organization, using as a pretext the invalid no-confidence vote, and misstating to the bank, the post office and others that the board of directors caused the problems with the organization's finances, knowing full well the members of the board, other than the terminated treasurer at no time had access to the bank account, books records or documents and things all of which had been under the sole and exclusive use and control of the terminated treasurer. In spite of being informed that this attorney could not have been hired by the treasurer as he claimed, because the treasurer had been validly terminated from the board, and in spite of being told the treasurer had committed this grievous malfeasance, which was more than likely going to leave the organization insolvent, the attorney proceeded to call a meeting of the members of the organization, not in accordance with the bylaws, to elect a new board of directors in order to not only protect the terminated treasurer, but to also reinstate the three terminated coaches, one of which was a child molester (as later discovered), another who had not had a valid coach's card for years, and a third who was the one left in charge when the other two decided not to come to work one day and resulted in six young girls being left alone on a military base at night next to a men's locker room for no less than fifteen minutes, in violation of the memorandum of understanding between the city, the swim team and the military base during a code orange. It was also discovered that eight Mexican Nationals had been transported on that base during that period of time when these coaches were employed and in charge, without obtaining special clearance as required for non-nationals, also during a code orange condition.

    To make a long story even shorter in approximately one month elections were held, and although the city initially did not recognize these individuals as a team because of their irregular actions, and because they had no valid legal corporate identity, the local swim team did nothing to help and eventually declared these individuals, all new to the team were the organization. Why? Because out of necessity, we were required to create a new corporate identity, separate from the swim team identity, not only for insurance purposed, but to keep the kids in the water. To them it only seemed fair, even though the $20,000.00 (twenty thousand dollars) they were able to get from the bank account as a result of this decision meant not a cent would be paid toward the debt now owed by the terminated treasurer for her failure to properly forward money taken from paychecks as withholding, (not the assets of the corporation) at all, even though an agreement had been reached with the State of California to place all the disputed funds in trust with the state to be held for the benefit of all creditors, a move that was not in the best interests of either the corporation or the terminated treasurer.

Unless you are very careful, this could happen to you. It is more common than you think. You cannot file for any kind of a bankruptcy if your organization is in suspension and debts incurred through fraud cannot be forgiven in bankruptcy, not to mention these were governmental debts. Even though I was negotiating with the IRS and the State of California, there was nothing I could do without the books, records documents and things, and I couldn't even go into court to get them because of the lack of legal standing caused by the suspension of the corporation.

Meanwhile, while the corporation was in suspension for the next three months, there was no valid insurance as two of the coaches that our board had terminated by a vote of three to one, the dissenting vote being the terminated treasurer, this group continued to claim the organization as their own, continued to coach, refused to cooperate in turning over the books, records, documents and things to assist in reviving the corporation as even paying the debt that caused the suspension could not revive the corporation without the paperwork completed that need to be filed, and this paperwork could not be completed without the information contained in the books, records, documents and things under the sole custody and control of the now terminated treasurer and her attorneys. As stated above, a legal action could not be filed in order to get subpoena power to get the books, records, documents and things, because there was no valid corporate identity, therefore the corporation had no standing to either bring a lawsuit or t defend itself in a court of law under the laws of the State of California. Hence, a legal quandary was created.

Everything You Never Wanted To Know About Your Nonprofit Corporation

Chapter Six

So What Did the Bad Guys Get? What Did They Do To Get What They Got?

Essentially the bad guys wanted to take over the organization and each of the bad guys had their own reasons for doing so, but what they ended up doing resulted in criminal acts, essentially, by not turning over funds as required to the governmental entities, they engaged in a continuing criminal conspiracy to defraud the state and federal governments, not to mention that this was money withheld from employee paychecks that if it was not due and owing the government, then it was the property of the employee. They have yet to be punished for these acts, and just maybe they will be able to convince the government(s) that since this was a kids' swim team they were totally ignorant of reporting and forwarding requirements. If this is the case, then what excuse do the attorneys the terminated treasurer hired have as lawyers are held to a higher standard of knowledge and therefore to a higher duty of care.

What is and was the responsibility of the board of directors who initially uncovered these acts? The duty of this board was to at all times act in compliance with the law, to try to rectify the problems, to have their counsel negotiate in good faith with the governmental entities in order to both protect the corporation and to do that which was right, even if it meant insolvency of the corporation and liquidation of the corporate entity all together. Ironically, the corporation could not even liquidate because it was in suspension at the time of the takeover masterminded by the terminated treasurer and the counsel she hired.

To this day the bad guys claim it is the fault of the board that discovered the problem that there were and are any financial difficulties at all, when the board that discovered the problem was not only a newly elected board, but was a board, like those before it that had no access or control over any bank account, books records, documents and things, and when they requested such access, the result was an immediate takeover of their organization.

This board worked under bylaws that should have protected them and that were sufficient to protect both them and the organization, but they did not protect anything at all. Why? Because the local sports organization that governed them and the national organization governing the sport never helped them or found in their favor. The climate towards them was openly hostile as they sought to "protect one of their own", the terminated treasurer a long time friend of many people of importance at the local level. Ironically, the local sports governing organization was also in suspension in the State of California and had no legal rights or standing under California law.

Never expect anyone to protect and help you. No one is there to protect you, your child, or your organization. Everything and everyone is sadly suspect. Everyone operates under their own agenda. That agenda is not always for good. If you decide to get involved, then it will all be up to you and your board to try to do the right thing, and it will not be either easy or simple. In fact, it may be hell. Be prepared for the worst, and then you can be surprised if everything turns out right.

So there you have it in a somewhat of an abbreviated nutshell. And when I say abbreviated, I mean abbreviated, because as hard as it is to believe there is indeed even more than this that has transpired. However, this is the essence of what you need to know as I lay out the groundwork stating how you can (perhaps) prevent this from happening to your organization; that is, if you are ready to take that huge and dangerous leap into the world of volunteering for any nonprofit corporation after reading all of this.

Remember, there is a very good reason people don't like lawyers, even though you may on occasions such as these need one.

Chapter Seven

Always Do the Right Thing and Please Sell Your Candy Bars, As Well as Other Related and Miscellaneous Matters

You should always do the right thing, even if everyone thinks you are wrong. Trust your instincts. Tell the truth and no one can ever say you are making inconsistent statements because the truth is always easy to remember. Expect everyone else to lie and for the lies to be believed. Expect to work very hard and for no one to appreciate you. Remember these are the same parents who would not buy a single candy bar during the fund raiser and they not only would not buy or sell the candy bars, they yelled at you for just having the idea to sell them. This is the joy of being a major player in the business of volunteering. Do not expect a single thank you for the "Tootsie Pop Tuesdays" you invented for the team kids, and you will either be sending out too much email or not enough email, be too informative or not informative enough. You cannot win. The minute you are gone, they will yell at you for not being there, and when you are there to chaperone the kids they will complain about how you do it. Drop your kid off and go home like they do, and just leave the job for someone else, or put up with it. Not all parents are nice people. Remember that. One coach told me that he loved working with the kids, but hated working with the parents, and that pretty much sums up the whole thing. It makes you wonder how those cute cherub acorn faces fell from those big ugly old oak trees.

However, you are not one of them or you would not be reading this book, so pay careful attention and learn something you can and will use.

So, you are in charge of the candy bar fundraiser, among a myriad of other things?

First, don't try to persuade any parent to move over to your point of view about anything, especially those candy bars. Don't. It will not work. Just hand them the candy bars with the written instructions and say nothing. Don't tell them it will build the character of their child or give their child a feeling about what it is like to be part of the team. Only your child believes that. They can buy them, sell, them, give them away so long as they hand you a check for the box of candy bars assigned to them to sell. There should be no excuses. At events parents who do not volunteer should pay a penalty, because no team can run on the small about of dues it collects and pay qualified coaches, and you don't want the cheap coaches or the volunteer coaches because they are probably child molesters, especially if they don't have a child on the team. Be suspicious of any coach who tells you they will coach for free. There are no free lunches and you need to generate money through fundraising to be able to keep your team numbers up and to retain qualified coaches because

qualified coaches cost money . Remember that it was your child who made half of the money collected for the Annual Swim-a-thon and no one ever thanked her for that. Besides, these people probably think you are rich and can make up the difference needed yourself and will gladly do so because their children are so wonderful, perfect and talented, and they will at the same time truly believe that everything you are doing you are merely doing for the benefit of yourself or your own child. Trust me.
This is how these people think. They will smile to your face and complain both behind your back and directly to you. Get used to it, because it's just the way life is in this warped world into which you have entered.

Remember asking someone to sell candy bars breeds hostility. If it is your idea they will not like it, and they will never have any ideas of their own, but they will be sure that you and your board are forcing them to do things against their wills and that everything you are doing is wrong, no matter how simple the idea and whether or not it happens to involve them at all. Just keep your mouth shut. They will like you better that way, and if they ask you why you aren't taking to them, say you have a headache and are not feeling well. (It is the truth after all, because they make you sick!)

The only place you are truly free to talk is at a closed board meeting. If a parent asks you where the team bylaws are, tell them you don't know and have them write a letter to the board requesting a copy, or post the bylaws on an internet site. You are not expected to carry bylaws with you or to have them memorized. Generally the law only requires that you have a copy available. If the person wants a copy of your bylaws, ask them for the costs of copying and tack on a handling charge for your time that you can put in into the team coffers. Always remember that as a board member of this nonprofit corporation you are a parent volunteer with a great deal of responsibility, and perhaps even liability, but you are not an indentured servant of these people and you personally owe them nothing. It will always seem like when you are working your hardest, they are complaining the loudest, and they probably are.

They will want to be at your board meetings and they will not care about federal privacy laws. They need to be at your meetings, especially if they are coming from outside of the community with a plan to takeover your team and the resources they believe you have that they do not have, whether it be pool or soccer field access, a perceived large bank account or the prestige of an exclusive team location address. In our situation the city was building a new and coveted swimming pool, it appeared we had a large bank account with adequate resources, (which we actually did not have due to the embezzlement), and we had what the bad guys considered to be a prestigious address. Everything about us screamed takeover

You need to remember all of this; and if someone is persistent in asking you for a copy of your bylaws, be suspicious, most normal team parents never ask for a copy of the bylaws. Trouble for your corporation may lie ahead. Remember if you have any kind of money in the bank and you are a parent owned and run corporation, someone will be after that money and/or in the very least have an express opinion as to what should be done with it, and if your club is located in an affluent upper class neighborhood, someone from the outside will most assuredly be looking in to get what you have, and will want to take it away from you.. It is bad. It happens. If the planets are all lined up properly everything could go absolutely wrong for you just as everything went absolutely wrong for us no matter how hard we tried to stop it. The sad thing about what happened to us is it hurt the children, and that was what we were all about, the children and nothing more, and nothing less. Is this not the purpose of any team sport, to serve the children?

Do not expect the locally governing sports organization to help you and do not expect the national governing body to help you either. If someone helps you thank your lucky stars because you will be miles ahead of anything we were able to accomplish.

We did manage to keep our kids in water and to continue, but we are still plagued by the outsiders who stole our corporation, its assets as well as its liabilities without taking responsibility for what was wrong about it or for any of its debts, leaving us to worry about our responsibilities from a legal standpoint, believing we must do everything in our power to protect our governmental and other creditors, or be subject to the responsibility for their debts in place of the corporation. It was required, necessary, expensive, time consuming and emotionally draining. This is why you do not want this to happen to you. This is why this book was written, to help prevent what happened to us from ever happening again.

This is a handbook of what you should and should not do and is by no means comprehensive or all knowing. As a lawyer I faced one brick wall after the next, never slept at night, devoted myself to the cause of right, and became sorely disappointed in the lack of common sense as well as integrity of the human race in general. However, the experience did separate the wheat from the chaff, the strong from the weak and the sincere from the insincere, and for this reason gave the experience intrinsic merit. Those of us who survived grew to value our children more, as well as the friendships between us; and this gave us some cause to celebrate the most minor of victories. The really stupid thing was that all this was really about was a kids' sport team. It was as stupid as the hockey parent (father) that killed another hockey parent (father), and served to point out how irrational some parents would be and could be as they lived their lives through their children instead of living their own lives for themselves. It was as stupid as the guy who worked for the boy scouts for thirty-nine years and who headed up a task force to prevent distribution of pornography to children, while he, himself, was allegedly distributing child pornography to children. As hard as it may be to believe, this stuff happens!

Chapter Eight

Kids Get Injured Every Day, So What?

You think you have hired a good coach and then he tells the kids to do something and they start coming up with stress injuries. Our coach had all the kids wear a drag suit for two full hours of swimming and a total of five to six thousand meters a day. Even the city lifeguards at the pool were complaining to the city about it but the city did not own the team so they ignored what they knew was wrong. You see, they only sponsored the team. After a while the strokes got shorter and the kids started rubbing their shoulders. My little Sally told me she thought the drag suit was hurting her about after two weeks of this ridiculousness and she talked to her godmother who was her open water swim coach (for distance ocean swim competitions).. Needless to say, the godmother was furious and this was way outside the bounds of as she put it "acceptable coaching", and was certain to cause stress injury even to the best of swimmers. The board talked to this coach and told him of their concerns as children were complaining of shoulder pain. The response was defiance and one of, "I am the coach and I will do as I please."

If this happens to you, what should you do? You hired him, you fire him, especially if he is signed to an "at will" contract. If you pay well, there will be plenty of coaches standing in line to take his place.

Most importantly, if your corporation is in suspension and an actual injury is claimed against your insurance and you are on the board of directors of the hiring corporation, then you may be held individually liable to the injured party. Yes, I know the kids' parents signed those waivers, but those are legally only worth the paper they are written on, especially in the State of California where technically a child may come back when he or she is eighteen and file a lawsuit of their own in regard to damages they have incurred. Also, waivers signed on behalf of minors are only a deterrent from a lawsuit and may put some contributory negligence upon the parent for allowing the activity, but they cannot really sign away the legal rights of the child. After all, a child is an independent being with his or her own legal rights

The point is that your board hired this guy and is responsible to make certain the children are safe and sound, and that does mean policing his coaching techniques, so be informed. You must act like the reasonable person and avoid foreseeable risk of harm, so if you see a coach doing something you think is wrong or if word comes to you about this and you hired this guy make him do the right thing. Make him act responsibly or tell him to get the hell out of there. This means you need to know what is right and acceptable as far as coaching standards are concerned. You need to know what is age appropriate for the child. An eight year old should probably not swim for two hours every day because his or her body is simply not ready for it, no matter how strong the child is. Even strong bodies wear out, and there is no reason your child should be in pain or crippled by the age of ten or any other child either, just so a coach or a parent can have a fleeting moment of glory.

In fact, in Australia they are totally revamping the way young girls and women are coached because of delay in menses and difficulty some women swimmers have had bearing children. The Australians have determined it is not wise or safe to overwork a young girl's body because that young girl may be damaged for life through over working out, eating disorders and/or improper coaching and the winning result is simply not worth the risk. I know of one coach who secretly gave his kids vitamins before practice and no parent or board member ever questioned this. Those vitamins were steroids. That coach quietly lost his team. I know this is true because I know a coach who was previously a swimmer who unknowingly not only took those vitamins, but who ended up with an eating disorder as a result of the influence and comments of this particular coach. This swimmer also, incidentally, had shoulder surgery at the age of twelve.

The point is, when you are on a board that owns a team, the buck stops with the board and you are it. You need to be vigilant. You can never let down your guard. Make sure you not only have a valid corporate status, make sure all the ducks are in a row. You may get sued individually even with a corporate veil, but without the veil you are left standing naked before God and the world, better yet the board should spend a bit more money and purchase insurance for its board of directors. If they care enough to have the fines, and you are the finest, then they need to pay for this. Then you can pass go, collect two hundred dollars and not lose the home you have come to love after all these years. No one said anything in life was easy. Do what you can, but don't be foolish. No one person is more important than you and your family, not even the arrogant, child molesting coach you mistakenly hired under (hopefully) an "at will" agreement, no matter what any of the other parents try to tell you.

If you put up with crap, it will be thrown back in your face. If you hired him, then fire him when he does wrong. You can trust a good coach, but do not give a bad coach a second chance. How do you know the difference? Ask your child. If your child comes home complaining about the workout, you know something is wrong. You just have to find out what that is. Educate yourself about the sport. You don't have to do it, just know it. Learn as much as you can and be informed. Read the sports magazines your sport publishes, ask questions, learn the rules, talk to your family doctor about what is good and age appropriate, and ask your national governing body for their age group guidelines and follow them. If you have your coach adhere to that, then at least liability will be lessened when and if a problem should occur. If you don't trust the coach and you can't get rid of the coach, leave the team and do not look back lest you be turned into a pillar of salt. Trust me. Even this, I unfortunately know from personal experience.

Remember when a child begins swimming at six years old, he has twelve more years of swimming back and forth across that pool before he gets to college to swim for four years more, and all he has to look at while he is swimming is a bláck line on the bottom of his swim lane. No matter what the sport is for the child, if it is to be long lived, don't wear it out—don't wear out the sport or the child! And please note that if you are a member of a governing board of a corporation that owns the team, you accepted responsibility with a grain of liability, so just take a deep breath and garner up your courage as there may be rocks on the road before you.

Kids pick their own heroes. My daughter wants to be that eighty-six year old guy that swims the mile at the ocean competitions and comes in dead last. If she wears her body out she won't be able to do that. Sometimes kids have their own ideas about what their goals are, and the best thing we can do as parents or as board members is to learn and to listen and to help them so they can kick that ball and run across that field and swim that Pacific Ocean mile at the age of eighty-six!.

Chapter Nine

How Could a Thing Like This Happen?

You are probably asking yourself how a thing like this could happen. How could an embezzling treasurer, a child molesting coach, a coach without proper coaching credentials and a group of people who came on to a team only three months prior to the take over, steal a swim team that had existed for many, .many years? The answer is, not without help and lots of it! Not only did the stars have to be properly aligned in the heavens, the bad guys had to get a lawyer who would do practically anything to further their position, one who did not care to check out the facts, and one who was able to properly massage the facts and change the timeline of the events to his own advantage, first saying a thing was so, and then by saying that it was not so—like the no confidence vote mentioned above, for example. Now even I, an attorney by profession, believed in the integrity of the United States Postal Service. Yet when these attorneys presented them with the no confidence vote they later admitted was void—the post office refused to turn over the United States Mail to the swim team. They held that mail for nearly thirty days until these attorneys called a meeting of members (and then beyond that until the takeover group ultimately got the mail), although they determined for themselves who was allowed to vote, so not all of the organization's members were noticed of this meeting, or entitled to vote, including two of the current board members at that time, and two additional families of which I am personally aware that had no notice of this meeting because they were also not entitled to vote for some unknown reason—You know, they were the ones who would disagree with the takeover. No one cared. The local swim committee didn't care. Somehow we were supposed to prove they did not notice everyone without any power of subpoena or discovery, rather than they prove that proper notice was given of this meeting. The same thing happened at the bank, and when the matter went before the local swim committee for hearing, they found in their favor because the post office found in their favor based upon a no confidence vote these attorneys later declared was null and void.

What all of them have not figured out yet is when you help someone with something like this (avoiding forwarding of money withheld from paychecks to proper governmental authorities, a felony offense) you become an accomplice after the fact; and no one wanted anyone to go to jail, but somehow the local swim committee decided what they did was OK and what I did was not OK. It was all my fault for giving wrong advice telling the board of directors to forward this money as required under law and to take all necessary steps to secure and to send whatever was owed to the proper authorities. Of course the board agreed with me. It doesn't take a brain surgeon to understand what had gone wrong here was very, very wrong. I was banned by them from volunteering for USA Swimming for three years, and the president of the board was banned for two, and we are proud of it because we did the right thing, no matter what the cost. The treasurer who had embezzled for years and who was a personal friend of those powers that be, received only a six month suspension from being a treasurer for a swim team, for failure to turn over books and records, and the terminated coaches without credentials (for now there were two) received 30 day and 45 day suspensions, not to be served at the same time. The child molesting and abandonment of children on a military base at night went entirely unmentioned along with the embezzlement. The treasurer was found to be the only one to bring. the corporation into compliance with the law by reviving it, even though she had caused it to be suspended for a period of over two years, and even though she and her attorneys had prevented the board of directors from reviving it by not turning over books, records, documents and things as well as the bank account and mail to which she had sole and exclusive access..

Now do I sound somewhat cynical? That is because I am. This was not good for the children, and it was not a good message to be sent to anyone. This is why I am telling you that what happened to us could happen to your organization unless your organization takes specific and necessary precautions.

If you are going to get involved in any nonprofit organization, make sure all the ducks are in order. Now. . . What are those ducks?

First duck should be your medical waiver with all necessary medical information on it, including who to call in case of an emergency and a right to authorize or administer emergency first aid. This should be kept with the coach at all times the children are present. If a child does not have a waiver on deck, he should not be allowed to swim.

Second duck should be a current team handbook updated yearly with everything any parent needs to know inside. This should contain sample healthy diets, how to dress and keep warm, where to obtain the team uniform, etc Healthy diet? You ask. Why .that? You need to include that to protect you so that if a child develops an eating disorder, the parent cannot blame the organization for the problem as the position of the organization as to a healthy diet has been clearly spelled out in the handbook.

Duck three is to inform your coaches they will not tell any child he or she is fat or overweight and/or to diet or to lose a few pounds for any reason whatsoever. Do not allow weigh ins of the children. A child should be able to eat any healthy food and this is the position the board must tell its coaches to take. Loss of a few pounds may make a kid run or swim faster, but a kid is a growing child and growing children should not be told to lose weight by anyone other than their parents or their doctor, and certainly not by an arrogant coach wanting to win another team trophy at the expense of the children. Don't even go near this liability doorway!

Fourth duck is to make sure the children have proper sports membership cards and allow only one day tryouts after which time membership cards in the national sports organization should be obtained and copies kept with the file with the coach. The reason for this is that the insurance the national organization provides may be void unless every participating child has a membership card. If a parent is not willing to invest in a membership card, you don't want their child on your team. It doesn't matter how talented the kid is, you cannot operate without insurance and if the card gives you that insurance, you need those cards. Check the specific rules of your sport in regard to this requirement.

Fifth duck? Enter into contracts with your coaches that are "at will", meaning they can be let go, fired, terminated and told to get lost and to never return, at any time for any reason. You should also set out with specificity exactly what you expect from your coach identifying what will constitute a breach of the contract as this will give you extra protection if the "at will" provision of the contract should be challenged for any reason and the contract has been breached..

The sixth duck is to look long and hard at your bylaws and if they give any doubt as to whether they will protect your organization, even if they have worked for years, amend them, and amend them with specificity. For example, do not allow anyone to serve on your board under the bylaws unless they have been a member of your team for at least one full year. This way what happened to us will not happen to you with a takeover by members who came on the team and were there for only a few months.

Duck number seven is to understand that the minute a parent starts to make trouble for your team, just invite them to leave. Don't spend any time with gypsies, tramps and thieves.

They will tell you they want to see the rules the minute you tell them they are breaking them, but they only want to see the rules so that they can argue with you and try to get the rules changed. Anyone who wants to see the rules before they will follow them has no intention of following the rules at all.

We had a kid pull down his swim suit and proceed to urinate on the poll deck. He didn't even bother to hide it in the pool. Then the board of directors was told by the coach it was all right because he was only ten years old. The board of directors did not agree. Even a three year old child knows better than to do something like that, and if the child doesn't know any better than to urinate on a deck and not in a bathroom, his parents certainly do and should promptly curb the behavior. No one should even have to mention this as a rule, much less clean up after this child. This child is not ready for a swim team. Even my little Sally was asked to leave a dance class when at the age of two she mooned herself in the mirror. We were politely told she could return in a few years when she was older and knew better than to do that, and she didn't even urinate on the dance floor! To me, this was normal two year old behavior, but to her teacher it was a shock as she had never encountered a child doing this in twenty years of teaching dance. Imagine what she would have thought of this ten year old boy urinating on her dance floor and exposing himself! Perhaps the boy had a problem and this was a cry for attention, but this was certainly not a problem for the board, nor one the swim team should have to accept.

For sanitary reasons and for other legal reasons, even an incident as small as this must and should be addressed. If you are a volunteer board member you will see and hear it all.

The point is you have to line up all of your ducks and keeping them in order will not be a simple task.

Now there is a somewhat happy ending to all of this. When the swim committee found against me, the opposition complained about me to the state bar, (and this was very upsetting as it was intended to be). After many hours of work and many sleepless nights, and the ultimate hiring of very competent counsel, I was vindicated and they said I attempted to accomplish the best for the swimming organization! I am very proud of this!

You see, even my very livelihood had been threatened by these people, and all because I volunteered to help a little swim team, and to give the IRS and State of California what was theirs.

Someone once told me the practice of law was not for the faint of heart, but no one warned me about volunteering for a nonprofit public benefit corporation. It seems this is the only place where you can work for free and lose your shirt.

Chapter Ten

Be a Duck! Or Just Act Like One!

Have you ever watched a gaggle of ducks? They are very cute. They just line up and go marching around. They are very organized. When a mother duck hatches her babies she takes them for a walk as soon as they are able to waddle, and those little ducklings just follow that mommy duck around all lined up like little toy soldiers. Wild ducks even fly in formation! So if you want to get your organization organized, you have to be a just like a duck!

Get the bylaws, and get all the bylaws. Get the bylaws of your organization, get the bylaws of the local sports committee and get the bylaws of the national sports organization. Get them on line, call and ask for them, or buy them. Also obtain every rule book and/or set of rules pertaining to how the different levels of the sport is run and determine exactly how the organizational make-up works from top to bottom. You are one of the ducks, but you fly in the back of the formation and not at the head, but as the feet, you still need to know what the head is doing and exactly what it is the head expects from the feet. The good thing about it all is that if nothing makes any sense to you about how things are done, you are the feet, so you can paddle away.

All right ducky feet what does this mean?

This means that in a perfectly healthy and normal situation everyone should be working together for the common good of the children, but please do not expect that! If you get that be surprised and be happy because your formation is flying high.

Sometimes when a mother duck takes her ducks out for a walk, the not so strong ducks stumble and fall down, and the mother just keeps paddling along and does not look back because she is interested in only the very strongest of the ducks. This is what happened to us. Those that were ahead of us carried power, and our mother duck was not interested if we stumbled and fell, and all the ducks in between just keep playing follow the leader walking around and around the barnyard. So it is important that you know all the rules and who is supposed to do what and the exact position all the ducks play in the formation of the sport, from top to bottom, or you will stumble, get up and then just stumble again and fall down and die.

You might be asking yourself why we did not go to court right away with all of this, and the answer is simple. First, remember we had no corporate entity because we were in suspension and therefore had no standing in a California court to either bring or defend a legal action; and second, we could not get the books, documents records and things necessary from the treasurer that we needed to revive the corporation so that we could get it into court. What we ended up with was a local swim committee that was also in suspension (although this was not known to us) deciding our fate. The national level determined that was all right because the local level got its authority from the national level, so they didn't need to have a valid corporate status at all because they were allowed to conduct a hearing in California under the authority of another state. The question before the local level was who was the corporation, us or the bad guys who were trying to get the $20,000.00 (twenty thousand dollars)

from the back that was all the property of the IRS and the State of California, and who ultimately did get that money as a result of decisions made by the local and national levels of the sport who refused to look at the withholding problem at all! In fact, I was found in contempt at the national level for trying to get them to address the problem and was fined $250.00 (two hundred and fifty dollars) as a result of my continued insistence the matter be addressed and for stating they were not looking at the matter with an impartial eye. For this I was admonished and told my comments were impertinent, Never mind if someone causes $30,0000.00 (thirty thousand dollars) to disappear from a bank account, and has not forwarded over $50,0000.00 (fifty thousand dollars) withheld from paychecks as required under law. Why, I was only trying to destroy the swim team according to them, not to do the right thing and save it!

Why did I do all of this? I did it to protect the corporation and the members of the board because it is always in the best interests of everyone to follow the law and not to advise the continuance of a crime. Ironically, all the time this was happening the board of directors was being told there was only about $8000.00 (eight thousand dollars) in that bank account, not twenty thousand dollars or more! Perhaps this little pad of $12,000.00

(twelve thousand dollars) was something just set aside for the benefit of the treasurer. This why of this is and was completely unknown to the board as moth after month the bankbook balance was stated as being in the eight thousand dollar range, and to this day it is unknown what actually was in that bank account because the board, including the president of the board as well as all the other board members could not even obtain that information from the bank because the terminated treasurer and her attorneys convinced the bank the board of directors was out to steal the money of the corporation, not to forward the money as required to the proper governmental entities, and they used that invalid no confidence vote to do it weaving a tale of deceit and deception so that they could all achieve their own personal needs. Their attitude was, "To hell with the IRS and the State of California! This money belongs to us!" The money simply went from the bank in a cashiers check to the last known address of the corporation, a post office box to which the terminated treasurer had "purchased for the corporation", and then using that admitted vote of no-confidence along with a letter from her attorneys, the board was forbidden access to the post office box.

All the board wanted to do was to send to the IRS and the state that money that was withdrawn from employee paychecks and was held in sacred trust; and it was not money owned by the corporation at all, but the property of another. This is why if it was not embezzlement before this, it became embezzlement now, and everyone who participated in the taking became a part of the act. What will happen as a result of all of these actions by all of these different people in relationship to the taking still unknown. I can only tell you that everyone in the chain was told the same thing. We wanted the money placed in trust with the State of California's Employee Development Department as they offered to do, so that all creditors could be noticed and make claim to what was theirs. Since there was no corporate entity when the agreement was made, and for that reason we could not put the money in trust with the courts along with the filing of a declaratory relief action, it seemed like the perfect solution as well as the perfect compromise to protect the corporation and even to protect the terminated treasurer as had everyone agreed it would have stood as an act of good faith toward restitution of what was taken.

The thing to take away from all of this is that you must remember that no good deed goes unpunished, and the doing of right has to be a reward in and of itself, even if it causes you expense, worry, sleepless nights, anger, frustration and depression. The sun will come out tomorrow, and if not tomorrow the day after tomorrow, so hold on tightly and swim as fast as you can away from the sharks out there in that murky water!

Check all the organizations at all the levels, determine their corporate status, obtain their bylaws and their articles of incorporation because in some states the articles of incorporation set out the framework of the organization and this may be helpful to you., and perhaps even necessary to have. Then make sure you know everything your organization needs to do to make certain its insurance cannot be voided for failure to take a step or two, and that if your organization is also an employer that your coaches are competent, certified and not child molesters! And do not forget to purchase workers compensation insurance for your employees. Our organization's embezzling treasurer forgot to pay for that as well. Luckily no employee was injured or because the corporation was in suspension that protective corporate veil was just not there! Imagine all the rain that could have come down on the heads of the board of directors had anything at all happened and a lawsuit been filed against the organization that could not legally respond and therefore would be found in default and automatically liable for damages! With thirty days to respond after service and no way to get the enormous amount of work done, especially with the treasurer and the attorneys she hired on behalf of the corporation after she was terminated refusing to turn over books, records, documents and things, this was a bomb ready to explode.

What do you do with a bomb? You diffuse it, you duck and cover, or you run away as fast as you can. You do not let the bomb fly with the flock. In our case we tried to do the right thing. We were lucky, no fatal injuries occurred, but the bomb exploded anyway, and there were some nonfatal casualties.

Chapter Eleven
Duck, Duck, Duck . . . Goose!

If you have discovered volunteering to be on the board of directors of a nonprofit corporation is like playing duck, duck goose because suddenly you are it, you are not alone in that game. Being it is not any fun especially if all you are trying to do is save something for the kids. In our situation the city who was a sponsor of our team stated it was their policy to not confer sponsorship on a youth team unless or until there was a valid nonprofit corporate entity, a business license and a 75% residency rule. As soon as the board hired the new coaching team, one of the coaches started stacking the team with non-residents of the city, some of whom even lived in Mexico. The city is small and contained and since the lifeguards grew up in the city they had a pretty good idea of who was a resident and who was not. The coach who stacked the team was told he could only bring fourteen swimmers with him and he actually brought twenty nine. The treasurer, (the one later terminated by the board), was also in charge of the team roster and she presented the board with a falsified roster that was given to the city. This roster was not complete and did not "match up" name for name with the records of who was on our team according to the local swim committee office. The board, without my advice determined it should tell the city the truth about the roster so that they would be acting in good faith, and so the roster was corrected. The coach was then told he must bring the membership of the team in line with the city requirement. This was the same terminated coach who thought it was all right for a child to urinate on the deck, and the same coach who thought it was all right not to show up for practice when six pre-teen girls were left alone on the military base for no less than fifteen minutes. This was also the coach who turned out to have reportedly had a sexual relationship with a minor he was coaching on the high school team from which he was ultimately required to leave. Of course the coach argued he had only brought fourteen children with him when this was obviously a miscalculation, to say the least, as there is an obvious and substantial difference between the numbers if fourteen and twenty nine; and it is difficult to hide an extra fifteen children recognizable as not being local residents, and not being the taxpayers who were footing the bill for either lifeguard or pool services. To top everything off six of those parents stormed the military base gate demanding access to watch their children and were escorted on to the base by the military Police. I was there and was asked if they had a way off the base and I told the military police that there was no way for them to get off the base, so they had to be escorted back off the base by the military police who had escorted them on to the base because they had told them there would be no problem and that they had simply missed their ride onto the base, all of which was completely untrue. To these people breaking this rule regarding military base entrance during a code orange and by storming the base was no different than breaking any other rule, and they all blamed me for the rules I never made. To transport parents on base would have meant shuttling them on and off and getting someone in the military to be with them and be responsible for them while they were on base. It also meant the children would not even get off the base until about 10 PM, because we had already tried that once and determined it was an impossibility and not good for the children. It was at that time I was accosted in the park an irate parent screamed at me, "We have a plan! We have a plan!" Besides, the attitude was that rules were not set in stone and merely meant to be broken, just like the law.

Shortly after that I began to worry that their plan was to take over the swim team. The only thing stopping them for the three months they were there prior to initiating the takeover was the membership application they had to sign to join the team that required a waiting period of three months prior to them becoming actual, full fledged members. Everyone who came onto the team had to submit the same membership application, but these were the only parents who complained about it. They complained about it because they had to wait three months before they could make their move to takeover the team. They were angry at having to wait, belligerent and self-righteous. As the situation became worse and worse one board member suggested that they be asked to leave, but the board as a whole kept thinking things would come under control and change. They didn't. If this ever happens in your organization, get rid of these people while you still can. This made the perfect set up for the terminated treasurer to garner support and the result was we lost the organization the IRS and the State of California were not paid and those who took the team also took a twenty thousand dollar bank account claiming it as an asset of the team when everything in that so-called asset was money withheld from paychecks of employees and not a team asset at all, but money that was legally the property of the IRS and the State of California, and if it was not, then the terminated treasurer had either misplaced, embezzled or stolen even more than those I represented were willing to charge against her, because they were going to put the entire twenty thousand dollars toward those debts even if it meant liquidating the corporation which they could not even do because the corporation was in suspension and in order to even liquidate a corporation you have to have not only a valid and existing corporation, but you also have to file a final tax statement, a factually impossible thing to do without books, records documents and things held and under the sole control of the terminated treasurer who refused to give these things to the board of directors as required not only under the law, but also under the bylaws of the corporation, It seemed as though things could not get any worse, but as you knew things just got worse and worse and worse.

What is the point of all of this? The point of all this is if someone can't follow the team rules and regulations, you need to invite them to leave the team. Better yet, when you hire a coach don't allow him to bring any kids with him from the team he is leaving. In swimming this is technically a recruiting violation by the coach, and although everyone does it, that doesn't make it right. Follow all rules to the letter and make a few rules of your own. If they come alone, then they won't have the power base to steal your team. If they bring a crowd, kiss your organization good-bye. Don't be tempted by the additional team revenue their dues may bring, because they may be the end of your team. Besides, it is recruiting and most so-called age group sports don't allow recruiting, even by a coach. Of course, our local organization didn't look at this as recruiting at all and decided instead we were recruiting by sending emails to our own team. Oh yes, and we, apparently stole our own website, a website that I personally paid for myself. It still befuddles me as to how we could steal that which was our own, how we could recruit our own swim team, and how money withheld from employee paychecks and not sent to the proper governmental authorities as required under law could be an asset of the corporation that the bad guys were ultimately allowed to take and spend with no intervention by anyone in the sport to make sure the money got to the place where it belonged, to its rightful owners, the state of California and the IRS, not to mention the additional money missing estimated to be another $30,000.00 (thirty thousand dollars).

So, if a coach wants to carry his own team over to your team, don't allow them to come; and if they come in flying in droves, send them away, or there won't be enough room in the duck pond for the original ducks; and the new ducks will just take over the entire pond, making it miserable for the nice little ducks that so innocently invited them to step into their pond. Besides, too many ducks make a big mess, and duck fights are not fun. You just end up with a lot of duck feathers everywhere, and the pollution is terrible, not to mention the smell.

Oh yes, and when you see a fifteen year old girl change on the pool deck against the rules that clearly state there shall be no deck changing of clothes, and she just stands there exposing herself in a black bra, tell her to get dressed and have some manners. Better yet, ask her to leave the team along with the ten year old boy who urinates on the pool deck rather than go into the bathroom with a chaperone as the team rules require.

Chapter Twelve

We Did the Only Thing We Could Do!

So there we were with a takeover group claiming they were us, going to swim meets and using the name of our organization, a group run organized and constructed by a wrongdoing treasurer and three coaches terminated, in part, for leaving children alone on a military base, unsupervised, for the second time. Now, of course, they deny that. They argue about the length of time that transpired, that the children were safe, etc., but I personally know they were left alone on that base because my little Sally was one of them, and she was scared and uncomfortable and her father was furious. The eighteen year old girl they argue was with them to keep them safe did not speak English, and this year she is listed on the swim meet sheets as being seventeen, which means she was only sixteen at the time!. Put quite simply, these three negligent coaches were assisted in a takeover of our team by the terminated treasurer who used the coaches (two of whom did not have valid coaching credentials during the two month period they took to revive the corporation) as a shield to hide behind. One of the coaches had even been fired from his high school coaching position for an inappropriate sexual relationship with one of his high school swimmers. Specifically, I was told his blue card was withdrawn and the determination was that it had been issued without sufficient prior investigation as there was a pattern of behavior that could be discovered by contacting previous employers (which to me meant this was not a solitary incident).

So what do you do if no one will help you get back a stolen corporation? What do you do if you cannot legally and validly conduct business because your nonprofit corporation has been stolen from you? I can tell you only what we did.

Our solution was to keep the swim team and to form a new nonprofit corporation to conduct the day to day business because without a valid nonprofit corporation the children would not have access to a pool.

Meanwhile those who masqueraded as our swim team and who were claiming the corporation as their own, most of them having been a member of the organization for little over three months, went about using the names of our vice president and president to obtain pool use, insurance, and to contact state and federal governments, even to somehow allegedly obtain powers of attorney that the IRS suggested I withdraw. When I asked the attorney hired by the terminated treasurer why they did this and if they did this, he screamed at me, "Of course they did! They had to, because you would not give us the corporation!" I kept telling the attorney that if he wanted the corporation he had to do things correctly, and he could not misappropriate the names of others to get the corporation because this was identity theft. It didn't ultimately make any difference to anyone, not to the local swimming committee or at the national level, but this was an extreme worry to those who believe and still believe they were and are the corporation stolen from them. And by the way, the second corporation was formed with the knowledge of the State of California Unemployment Development Department who which was the one who offered to put the funds in trust for the benefit of governmental and other creditors. There was no possible way this board was going to defraud anyone. Besides, there actually were no taxes to pay, and the opposition was correct in that, What had happened was a taking of funds belonging to another, namely to the state of California and the government of the United States as these were funds withdrawn from the paychecks of the employees and part of their gross earnings. In essence the theft was from the employees as well as the governmental entities. Why should we characterize this as a wrongful taking? If this was not a wrongful taking and merely a mistake, then why would the terminated treasurer need to hide behind the terminated? Coaches and hire attorneys in the name of the corporation to take over the corporation to prevent the duly elected officers of the corporation from doing anything to her because those elected officers would lack legal standing if they were no longer the officers of the corporation. Therefore, they would have no valid legal complaint as representatives of the corporation, incorporated or not.

  Think this treasurer may have been innocent? Well, think again, because ten years earlier she took this position from another treasurer who did not forward withholding to the IRS and who had also misplaced money from a snack bar money box, and it was the treasurer terminated by our board who apparently allegedly negotiated and talked to the IRS and others to resolve the matter. The other treasurer made payments and paid back the money to her board, and when she missed only one payment the treasurer our board had terminated for those same acts, signed a paper and was willing to file a complaint against her predecessor with the city police. Perhaps she took lessons from her predecessor and made a few improvements on the scam because she got away with it for far longer than her predecessor. The point is that she knew what she was doing and she knew what had to be done. Maybe it was the thrill of the taking, or maybe she thought she was preserving the swim team by keeping her secret; however, the IRS in recent ruling has made it clear if the one who writes the checks does not make the quarterly payments, they will be held personally liable for those payments even if the employer has directed that employee to withhold payments. In a recent case before the IRS an employee who quit her job because of this in and later reported the problem to the IRS was held responsible and liable to the IRS because she was in charge of the checkbook and the IRS held it was her responsibility as an individual to make certain the payments were made in a timely fashion.

Because no one apparently knew the law in relation to all of this, the twenty thousand dollars in the organization's bank account was not put in trust with the State of California Unemployment Development Department, and the attorneys hired by the terminated treasurer refused to send anything to the governmental entities without giving justification or excuse, and now it would appear the terminated treasurer will be held liable for twenty thousand dollars more than she would have owed had the government at least been given that twenty thousand dollars.

What did those who were taking over the organization say? They said the governing board was out to steal their money. Money they never earned, in a corporation in which they had no long term vested interest. They also said the corporation created to keep the kids in the water swimming was only created to destroy the corporation they now claimed was theirs, and ultimately the local swimming committee agreed with them.

What the local swimming committee and national level did not understand was that they had authority over a swim team and not over a California corporation that was separate from the team; however, because they got the word from a post office paralegal that was based, in part, on that invalid no confidence vote that the duly elected board of four months who had discovered and uncovered this problem, was not the board of the organization, the swimming committee relied on that opinion and made its own predetermined opinion on long term friendships and relationships with the terminated treasurer that she and only she could do the right thing. Suddenly everything was turned around and it was the duly elected board that was somehow taking over its own corporation, and not merely taking its own corporation back. All of these things just kept snowballing so that by the time it was all done, and the corporation was revived it quickly became to late to do anything to recover the twenty thousand dollars and to get that money to the IRS and to the state where it belonged, not even one penny of it. Throughout all of this our message was clear. We did not want the money in the bank account for any other purpose than to place it in trust for the benefit of governmental and other creditors, yet even the local swimming committee decision stated we were after assets that we never claimed for any purpose except to give back what was clearly not the property of the corporation, as it was money withheld from paychecks in a sacred trust to be turned over for income tax withholding, social security payments and the like that was never sent to its proper end.

The problem is that if a local committee says it has power over your California Corporation and nothing is done about this at the national level, then everyone believes them, and then if the local level orders your attorney cannot even represent you or any other swim team now or in the future, as is what happened to me, your organization is pretty much left without a paddle to go up the creek, especially since attorneys fees and court cost are quite expensive. It feels like hitting a brick wall, especially if you are a volunteer only trying to do the right thing.

Most people on the outside could not believe what had happened to us, and as unbelievable as all of this sounds. all of this is true, and this is all only part of the story, a story with so many twists and turns that .all we can now hope for is that someone else will read this handbook and will learn from our experience so that this could never happen to them.

To those who did this or to anyone who has done something similar to someone out there, I say shame on you because you have hurt people who loved and trusted you and were just trying to help you, and you are in need of help

If you intend to protest this writing, then I say, "Go and write your own book and get it published. Stop burying your head in the sand like an ostrich, stop hiding behind trees in the forest, and come out of your hole in the ground, for you are nothing but a snake who steals from little children and anyone who is with you is the same as you and knows no better and deserves our pity along with our prayers. If you have done this or anything like this to anyone, it is not too late to come out into the sun. It is never too late to do the right thing. The sun could come out tomorrow if you would only come out of your holes".

Oh yes, and thank you for buying my handbook.

To the rest of you innocents, please take heed if this is happening to you; and if it is not happening to you, .then take the steps set forth in this handbook and perhaps, just perhaps you can prevent happening to you what happened to us. While I can only hope our story is now over, it may still be that an addendum could be added to this book, and the whole thing is stupid, and nothing less than stupid, because all this is about and was about is a kids' sports team. This should have been only about what was and is best for the kids and in the best interests of the swimming organization, and that should have been to follow the law and to give the money in the bank account to the governmental entities whose property it clearly was. No one should continue in the furtherance of a crime, and no attorney should assist a client in the furtherance of a crime. Since not forwarding money withheld from paychecks to those for whom the money was withheld is a criminal act, to not agree to forward that money even after the fact is to continue the criminal act. It was as one parent put it, "much ado about nothing." (He was fighting cancer and could easily put it all into perspective.)

All that had to be done was the right thing, and even if you do not believe the truth when you hear it, a reasonable person hearing something provable or disprovable through a few phone calls should pick up the telephone and find out for himself or herself where the truth lies. All the alleged newly elected president of the organization had to do was to make a phone call or two and ask a few questions in order to ascertain the truth. As I said earlier in this handbook, believe no one and check out everything for yourself. No one ever had to believe me because they had the means to find out for themselves, but they chose not to exercise those means.

The question is, why did they all believe them? If that newly elected president of the corporation, reads this, perhaps he will make those phone calls instead of believing everything and anything anyone from the dark side tells him.

. I have told everyone who to call about everything, and I have even published phone numbers as well as names of who to call in my quasi judicial hearing papers and pleadings, but in at this point in time, as then, no one cares about the truth at all.

The attitude of the sports organization at both levels was and is that they simply will not and would not address the IRS problem and the other related matters, and if the government wanted its money it could go and get it.

I can only wonder if they bother to file and pay their own yearly state and federal taxes, or if they would be upset if someone withheld money from their paychecks as payment towards their taxes, etc. and just kept that money and didn't forward it as required under law.

What would happen if suddenly they had to collect social security disability and nothing was there from which they could collect? Even if social security is not a bank, if you never pay I into it, when you need it is not there. This is why the department of social security sends out statements that show how much was paid into it on your behalf and asks to you notify them if anything is incorrect. It is up to you to notify them if something is wrong, and it will be up to you to prove money was withheld from your paycheck and sent to them on your behalf and that is why they ask you if the social security earnings as set forth on their statement are correct. The amount you collect is also proportional to the level of earnings put in, so if nothing is there fir four or five years and you become disabled and unable to work you want every penny withheld on your behalf to be there and you don't want to have to go to the trouble and possible legal expense to prove anything at all to them. If you have a husband or wife and children depending on your social security disability income or even on your social security death benefits, (God forbid), you want that money there and you don't want to have to go looking for W2's to prove you worked for John Blowhard or anyone else.

    I tried desperately to get this matter addressed by the national level because this was an important issue to one of our coach employees and so it was important to us, even after they refused to do so, because for us, this was the essence of our complaint. We were told nothing would be addressed that was not ruled upon at the local level, rendering our appeal to the higher level useless, so we withdrew the appeal ourselves as the appeal would only take up time and expense and we were clearly told our appeal issues would never be addressed. Then I tried to file a complaint against the local level with the national level because they were in suspension and had no legal right to act and was told they were acting under the national corporation. My complaint against them was ultimately dismissed by the national level without a hearing and/or opportunity to be heard. When I persisted in bringing up the withholding matter, asking that it be considered because this was an important and issue central to our case, I was told I would again be found in contempt and required to pay another $250 (two hundred fifty dollars) if I ever brought up the matter again or even contacted the hearing officer. My complaint had been dismissed. I was told in writing that everyone up the ladder of control agreed with him, and the exact positions were named, making any further appeal futile, as well as a waste of time, money and expense. Trying to do the right thing can get quite costly. So I decided to write this handbook instead, especially since my hands are now apparently tied with the order banning me from volunteering for any swim organization for a period of two years, something neither legal or ethical as it limits my ability to practice law and was decided by a chair who was a member of the state bar through agreement with the four other members of the hearing board, but it is something not worth the expense of fighting, because I must have been insane to volunteer in the first place and I have now done everything I can possibly do to try and get the governmental entities what was withheld from paychecks and what is theirs.

    All we can say is that at least we tried to do the right thing, and we have the paperwork to prove it. If this happens to you, make a paper trail of your good faith efforts. That way you will become a witness, and not an accomplice or a participant in the continuance of criminal acts.

    It is sad, but it is true that sometimes your friends will not listen to you when you try to get them out of trouble, and that they may even turn and attack you for trying to help them. I suppose it is true that what is right and what is wrong all depends on how you look at it, but there is a reason that laws have been created, and there are reasons for doing right. Why play Russian roulette with a loaded gun if someone is willing to help you get out of trouble for free? Don't ask me, because I am just the wrong person to ask. Once you get into the pond you either sink or you swim.

"Well, Ollie, what a fine mess they have gotten themselves into now!"

Everything You Never Wanted To Know About Your Nonprofit Corporation

Chapter Thirteen

Why Didn't We Just Give Them the Corporation?

Why didn't we just give them the corporation when we started the new corporation? The answer is that we tried to do just that. In fact we tried more than once. I was authorized to make an offer of settlement when the opposition revived the corporate status prior to the decision as to who should allegedly have the corporation. Although we considered them interficious intermeddlers in reviving the corporation they had taken from us, the decision was made to offer them the corporation because by now, at the behest of someone at the local swim committee, we had also started a new swim team. Part of the offer was that the bad guys were to take the assets as well as the liabilities of the corporation and relieve the board members who had discovered the acts of malfeasance from liability for debts caused as a result of the malfeasance. The offer included the stipulation that the agreement made between the state of California Unemployment Development Department and our board to place the bank account in trust for the benefit of governmental and other creditors be honored.

The bad guys were very angry that were able to continue operating and even tried to get the local committee to take away our team because they stated that by us continuing we were out to destroy the original corporation. We argued that this position was without merit because we still believed we were the original corporation, otherwise we would have not made the offer to transfer the original corporation to the bad guys with the caveat they honor the debts and liabilities of the corporation as well as the assets. Besides, when the second corporation was created the first one was in suspension and did not exist, and the bad guys were preventing the good guys from reviving the corporation, because they thought if they revived it themselves this would mean it was theirs.

The local swimming committee board of review decided ultimately that I personally was out to destroy the original corporation when I formed the second corporation at the request of the good guys who only wanted to keep the kids of the community in water. They did not consider that there was no valid legal identity of the original corporation when the second corporation was incorporated because the first was in suspension. This is probably because they were themselves in suspension, a fact not shared at the so-called board of review hearing. Even though the committee decided the second corporation was created to destroy the first nonexistent corporation and not to keep the children in water, they did not take away the creation of the new swim team, and they could not take away a valid California corporation, even if they may have wanted to do just that. They could, however, take away counsel for the board of directors by banning me from acting as an attorney for any swim organization for a period of three years, at least they believed they could, and so they did. Even though they had no valid legal jurisdiction over me, (which was admitted in the findings), because I was not a member of the good guys board or a member of the local or national swimming organization. I was banned from even selling a hot dog in the team snack bar, not to mention curbing my right to practice law for any other swim organization, pro bono, retained or otherwise, and the president of our corporation was banned form volunteering for a period of two years, something he really did not mind because it meant he did not have to serve as a swim official at swim meets from seven in the morning until four in the afternoon on swim meet weekends. An appeal was taken as stated above, and there were legal actions through the post office in attempts to get the check to the proper governmental authorities, all to no avail. Each hearing officer relied on the poor prior findings of the one before him, beginning with the paralegal at the post office and that admittedly invalid no confidence vote used by the attorneys hired by the terminated treasurer without authorization of the organization. No one looked at this as a whole, and every decision was based upon a narrow part of the whole. The result was an injustice, and the continuing commission of a crime to defraud governmental agencies of what belonged to them. The best thing for everyone would simply have been to put that money in trust for the benefit of governmental and other creditors, and then to have worked negotiate payment from there. This would have been in the best interests of everyone, but this is not what happened. Oh yes, the embezzling terminated treasurer was give a six month suspension from serving as a swim corporation treasurer, but she could still sell hot dogs. The coaches without coaches cards were suspended for thirty and forty-five days, not concurrently, with the molestation issues ignored.

So what happened to the offer that we made to give them the corporation way back when the bad guys prevented us from reviving it so they could revive it themselves and then steal it?

The offer was refused with the caveat that the bad guys would investigate the liability of the good guys' board members making this offer for not conducting the business of the corporation in a proper manner. Remember, these board members had been on board for only four months when irregularities were discovered; and the only one who ever had books, records, documents and things as well as access to the bank account and checkbook was the treasurer they had terminated by unanimous vote for doing these things.

Somehow the attorneys hired by the terminated treasurer without authorization of the organization, the very counsel who organized a meeting and takeover vote of the corporate board, were now saying those who requested the books, records, documents and things for independent audit and to revive the corporation and who were so refused, were somehow responsible that no independent audit was made of those books, records, documents and things, that they, themselves, refused to have turned over to this board for such an audit and revival of the corporation. These attorneys alleged, and the local swim committee found that this board and I had done nothing to revive the corporation, a finding completely unsupported by the evidence presented, and upon which no independent investigation had been made in spite of names and phone number and contacts given to that reviewing board, both orally and in writing, that clearly proved otherwise. It made no difference that the good guys had no access to the bank account, and even if the good guys had paid the debt due to revive the corporation; they did not have the books, records documents and things necessary to fill in the papers that were required to be filed to revive the corporation. Somehow this debt was perhaps confused with the other withholding matters. The bad guys' attorney said there was no problem at all with the IRS, when a phone call by our board president to the IRS the day before the hearing (which was testified to under oath that day) proved otherwise. The same thing applied to the State of California Unemployment Development Department. Somehow it was perceived that the good guys had to have some sort of bill to prove anything was due and owing anyone. Of course this was not a requirement for responsibility. . Do you get an annual bill from the IRS? The answer is no. You are expected to file your tax returns and pay your taxes when due. Of course no income tax was due and owing the IRS or the State of California because this was a tax exempt organization (when revived), and there was no income tax taxed upon it. This was money withheld from paychecks of employees in trust. It was not the property of the corporation. This made the situation what is was, and what it is, a crime. It was nothing more and nothing less. These were bad guys, and they were hurting the most innocent among us. They were hurting children. They stole a swim team and a corporation from a group of children.

The arguments of the bad guys were ludicrous. Their arguments were absurd. The good guys were left in the position of having to do everything they could to make certain that funds that were there in the organization's bank account, but never under their control, and in fact were prevented by unauthorized hired counsel from obtaining, were forwarded to the governmental entities to which they belonged; and they would have that responsibility as long as they were the valid board of directors, and until it was deemed otherwise, and unless and until they took every step reasonable and legal to make certain governmental entities could get what was theirs, and not the property of the corporation.

In spite of saying over and over again that the good guys didn't want the money and that it was all due the governmental entities and others and that good guys wanted to put the funds in trust as stated above, the finding of the local swim committee board of review was that the good guys wanted the assets to enrich the new corporation!

None of anything that was happening made any sense at all, and everything was spinning out of control.

The point is once you began an act, you owe a duty of care in that act, and you must do everything possible according to the reasonable man standard of care to avoid foreseeable harm to another, or in the very least you may be found negligent in a court of law.

The corporate rule of law is when one takes a corporation as their own, they accept the assets of that corporation along with the liabilities of that corporation, thus releasing those who preceded them in the corporation. In a nonprofit corporation there are no shareholders. There are no shareholder derivative lawsuits. However, there are assets and liabilities and certain responsibilities that must be accepted by the successor to the corporation. Therefore, the buyer or the taker should beware. In this instance, the bad guys wanted to accept the corporate assets, but not the liabilities, and were, in fact, threatening former board members with a civil action saying they were responsible somehow for the acts of the terminated treasurer over whom they had no control.

It is also true that when and if a legal action is filed by either the IRS or the State of California in regard to those funds not forwarded, that those entities that file will more than likely name all the boards of directors individually from the beginning of the malfeasance. They have to do this to sort out the chaff from the wheat, and at that point in time if you have not become a part of the solution, you become a part of the problem.

In other words, the best thing to do was and always is to be a part of the solution, and this means doing everything possible to see to it that money withheld from paychecks goes where it is supposed to go, and that all corporate rules are followed as well as all applicable law.

Be only a witness .to a criminal act, and do not become a participant in it. You may still be named in a civil action, but if you have done everything in your power to get the money where it is supposed to belong, and if you have done everything to protect what is right and good under the law, then you will not only have a valid civil defense, you will also have a defense from any criminal act.

Sometimes no one gets it, no matter how many times you tell them, even in writing, even when you spell it out in writing to opposing counsel.

To all of you I say, "Volunteer at your own peril and please look before you leap into the fire!"

By the way, did you see "The Simpsons" (cartoon) episode where Homer Simpson was the winner of corporation in a poker game. The CEO of the corporation let Homer win the corporation because the corporation was in trouble. Homer thought he was rich, but he ended up going to jail because the previous CEO, who owned the corporation and who had tricked Homer into winning it in the poker game, had engaged in shareholder fraud. As Homer was being carted off to jail, Homer said something like, "I forgot! I got the liabilities as well as the assets of the corporation when I won this corporation! I thought I was rich, and now I have to go to jail! I was tricked! I was tricked!" Homer eventually got out of jail when the former CEO confessed to the whole thing and to tricking Homer. The point is, even a cartoon character knows the law. When you get a corporation you end up with both its assets as well as its liabilities

Chapter Fourteen

The Good, The Bad and The Ugly

In order to protect your organization before the bad guys come rampaging in, you need to check out everything and then get your paperwork into order. If you find you are in suspension as we did, and if the cause of the suspension is a possible or actual embezzlement, then you must put away your personal feelings of friendship for this person and report the situation to the local police immediately when and if you receive in return for your inquiries nothing less than candor, truth and an immediate turning over of the books, records, documents and things. Our board only hesitated, and then decided to wait and see if the local or national level of the organization would help in correcting these matters, and everyone just ended up losing. No one wanted to listen to me, and I wasn't even listening to myself, because if I had been listening to myself I would have done everything in my power to see to it this problem was reported to the authorities immediately, because as soon as the treasurer was able to dummy up that invalid no confidence vote, (a vote without a quorum or sufficient members in good standing voting), and one person and/or entity after the next believed this document as valid when the hired attorneys either knew or should have known this document was invalid as they later admitted, it became impossible to convince anyone of anything. Everywhere we went we were met with a challenge as to our standing to do anything; and this was another reason, besides the corporation being into suspension, that we needed to create a new corporate identity. When the new corporate entity was created I called it giving birth, because we had crested an entirely new legal identity. It was an identity that could validly conduct business and that could keep the kids in the water. The board hired world class coaches with valid coaches' credentials through a swimming school, which meant they were independent contractors and the new entity would not have to do any withholding from paychecks because all the legal stuff would be through the school. It simplified matters, but we were still under attack by those whole stole our corporation in the first place, and we were still left with the legal and moral obligation to do that which was correct and right. This was not something the board agreed to do because they were told to do it by an attorney. This was something the board of directors who were the good guys wanted to do because it was good, just and proper.

  This handbook will begin now at the beginning of the creation of the nonprofit organization, and the documents presented can be viewed in relation to where your corporation is, with the caveat that this is the advice and general opinion of only one person who happens to be an attorney, and it is not intended as specific advice, and that if you or your organization have any particular question on any area of the law, independent legal counsel should be sought as laws differ from state to state.

You may also want to get more than one legal opinion as legal opinions may differ. I, personally, would never have believed anyone who was an attorney could have advised the terminated treasurer and the rest of the bad guys to go in the direction they went, and I would never have believed they would have gone so far as to participate in it or that anyone would have ever taken their position as it was so contrary not only to our organization's bylaws, but also flew in the face of the law. I am to this day trying to determine why they all did what they did, and why they participated in this takeover, never offering or considering resolve, while refusing offers of settlement along the way. They got what they wanted, but at what price?

Is getting what you think you want ever worth the price of your soul?

I am the attorney who tells her clients it is best to accept responsibility for wrong, even if it means going to jail. My clients do not tend to be repeat offenders, get help if they need it, because I help them get help; and sometimes if they end up doing a bit of jail time, I am even thanked for sending them to jail. One young drug offender told me it was the best thing that could every have happened to him.

Stealing is not unlike the taking of a drug.

If you are an attorney reading this, the best thing you can do is to help your client get the help he or she needs. It is not in your client's best interest to help in the continuance of wrong. Read Dostoyevsky' classic novel, "Crime and Punishment", and then help your client to do the right thing. Don't convince your client there is somehow some other explanation for their wrong, and don't blame the fact they were trusted and beloved; and therefore they were not questioned soon enough and discovered in their wrongdoings by those who trusted in them. It is not always just about the win. In other words, if someone does a wrong thing, it is not the responsibility of one who did not do the wrong thing to catch the wrongdoer in it and then to make it right. In fact, under California law, a board of directors is entitled to rely upon the representations of their fellow board members and will not be held liable under the laws of the state of California for so relying.

When children are involved, it is important to set an example. Do what is right. If you do what is right, the example can never be wrong.

Chapter fifteen

The Articles of Incorporation

After forming an organization that decides to have a nonprofit entity so that they have a corporate veil under which the organization may work while protecting the members of the organization as well as the board, the first step is twofold. Choose and reserve a corporate name and create and file the articles of incorporation.

After choosing the name of your corporation and reserving it if required to do so by your state, then you can write the articles of incorporation. Each state may have its own requirements as to what these articles of incorporation may have to say, from the very simple to the more complex. You can sometimes find out what is required by following on line examples offered by your state, you can look in a nonprofit handbook written specifically for your state, or you can look in your state codes.

The articles of incorporation for the State of California are very simple, and they can be walked through by counter delivery in about two days, if you live in an area of California where there is a local branch office of the California Secretary of State. You can find an example of what these are supposed to look like on line at the California Secretary of State's website. You only need to copy these form articles and fill in the blanks and then follow the directions for over counter or mail in fees. If you incorporate over the counter in California you will have your articles stamped and ready to go in two days. The state will give you a certain amount of time to file you statement of information. In California this is a separate document with a separate fee and names the officers of the corporation along with the agent for service of process. Since this is a corporation and not an individual, then an individual must be named in the articles stating who may accept service of process (a lawsuit, summons and complaint or other legal notice, such as a notice of suspension). In the instance of our corporation, the terminated treasurer had also been listed on the statement of information as the agent for service of process, so all notices of suspension had gone directly to her and were ignored by her, and she did at no time advise any board under which she served that the organization was even in suspension, putting the organization in direct peril as stated above. It is for this reason you should not trust your agent for service of process to actually tell you anything; and while a lawsuit may be hidden, suspension is something you can check out on line; and had the organization checked this out and done this early on in the approximate four year suspension, the problem may have been able to be both stopped and resolved before it got out of hand as it did.

Also, you should note that if you are doing substantial business in a state other than in that state in which your organization is incorporated, then you may need to file within that state as a foreign corporation in order to do business within the state. In our instance the local swimming committee had been in suspension for approximately four years. Upon this being reported to the national level it was determined the local swimming committee was acting under the authority of the national governing body. Since this had been apparently going on for a period of four years, it was probably necessary to file for foreign corporation status in order to sustain this legal argument. This was not done and had heretofore gone unchallenged. It is also interesting to note that the conclusion was that they were acting under the laws of Ohio in California under the national corporation which was also incorporated in the State of Colorado. Apparently there were two corporations under which they could operate, and the reason for this is unclear. The national committee is located in Colorado so that it makes sense for incorporation to be there, as in the least it would seem like they would have to file as a foreign corporation within the state in which they resided if the laws of Colorado were anything like the laws of the State of California. This mystery, however, will be left for another attorney and another day.

The bottom line is that your local and national organization will pretty much do whatever it wants to do based upon what they perceive is in their own best interests. In our case it is shocking, but true that so much of what we were trying to do to preserve the integrity of the corporation was ignored, and both the local and the national governing bodies were on notice every step of the way as to every single thing that was done, and at each juncture of every step there was a plea to help us and guide us and to tell us what was right, and all of this was ignored, until suddenly there came the hearing, nearly five months after the fact with a hammer dropped upon our heads.

So, with that background in mind, here are our articles of incorporation, with all the names removed, for obvious reasons. Please remember that these may not be correct to use in your state and not only use the resources set above, but also check with your own legal counsel for specific advice.

To follow is what the State of California requires for beginning any nonprofit corporation; and this document along with required fees is all you need to begin the process once you have ascertained no one else is using the corporate name you have chosen as your own; and with search engines you can check through your state's website to see what corporate names are in use, although you cannot see which corporate names are reserved, so if you want to take a chance and skip the reservation process, the very worst that can happen to you if your corporate name choice has been taken is that if you file over the counter in a two day process, you will be refused filing and told to get another corporate name.

Basically, all you have to do is to fill in the blanks and write a check for the appropriate amount, make sure you are filing in the correct category and that you qualify to be a nonprofit corporation; and in two days your nonprofit corporation is on its way. Next, y0ou will need to fill out and send in the Statement of information with those fees, but that document will come attached to your articles of incorporation if you are in California and you will be given a date upon which the initial statement of information must be filed. You can mail that in, and then immediately upon receipt of the approval of the articles of incorporation get your federal identification number with which you can open a bank account and begin business. You will also need to comply with local rules that may require you to file for a business license where the business if being conducted. Specific rules and requirements will vary from state to state and from city to city. Check with your state and local authorities, and consult legal counsel.

ARTICLES OF INCORPORATION
Article I

The name of this corporation is:
- A. This corporation is a nonprofit **PUBLIC BENEFIT CORPORATION** and is not organized for the private gain of any person. It is organized under the Nonprofit Public Benefit Corporation Law for **public and charitable** purposes.
- B. The specific purpose of this corporation is:

Article II

The name and address of the person for initial service of process is:

Name:

Address:

City: State: Zip:

Article III

- A. This corporation is organized and operated exclusively for **charitable** purposes within the meaning of Section 501(c)(3), Internal Revenue Code.

- B. No substantial part of the activities of this corporation shall consist of carrying on propaganda, or otherwise attempting to influence legislation, and the corporation shall not participate or intervene in any political campaign (including the publishing or distribution of statements) on behalf of any candidate for public office.

Article IV

The property of this corporation is irrevocably dedicated to **charitable** purposes and no part of the net income or assets of this

corporation shall ever inure to the benefit of any director, officer or member thereof or to the benefit of any private person. Upon the dissolution or winding up of the corporation, its assets remaining after payment, or provision for payment, of all debts and liabilities of this corporation shall be distributed to a nonprofit fund, foundation or corporation which is organized and operated exclusively for **charitable** purposes and which has established its tax exempt status under Section 501(c)(3), Internal Revenue Code.

_____

(Signature of Incorporator), Incorporator

Everything You Never Wanted To Know About Your Nonprofit Corporation

Chapter Sixteen

**Writing Your Bylaws
Or Changing Them to Protect Your Corporation**

If your bylaws do not protect your corporation from being stolen, then they are absolutely worthless. Even if you have good bylaws that should protect you, look at them again. You need to make certain that the bylaws are absolutely takeover proof, and if someone comes to your organization and starts to complain about them, then tell them to just go away. Make sure your membership requirements as well as your bylaws setting forth membership requirements as well as any qualifications to serve are very specific, and either stagger board of director positions and when they can be replaced, or make the terms long enough so that a takeover cannot be easily accomplished. The problem with our organization was that not one single doting, complaining parent ever wanted to serve, so it was pretty much if you agreed to take on the esponsibility to be on the board of directors, you were actually elected until you decided to leave; so while the president of the board and others went in and out from year to year, the embezzling treasurer remained on the board for years, trusted, while she made her insidious moves. She served as an official, organized the snack bars and appeared to work in a selflessness fashion for the organization. However, appearances, as we found out were deceiving, and the actions that transpired after the discovery of what had happened were by no means selfless, but were orchestrated for self preservation.

This is they key. No one does something for nothing, and there is no free lunch. Even when one serves, one serves for his or her own purpose, whether it is to help one's own child within the sport, to garner some sort of perceived prestige in the community, or to just have that feeling of feeling good for doing something good. Sometimes ill motives of power, greed and need to take advantage of the weak, young and helpless are involved. Some parents only want a ribbon or a trophy or a medal to place on the mantle, and because they believe the bad guys can get this for them, they just simply go along with the flow. Some parents don't care at all because the team is merely a babysitting service and if girls are getting molested and they have boys, it doesn't matter the coach has had an inappropriate relationship with a minor. They fail to recognize that anyone in a position of authority anywhere who takes advantage of another sexually, even as in the workplace between employee and employee, between even adults who have authority over other adults is wrong. Where outrage would be considered on one hand, when it comes to our children, outrage is often woefully missing.

To follow is one example of a set of bylaws. They are not perfect and were written in an attempt to prevent another takeover of our newly created corporation, the one created to keep the kids in water while we attempted to revive the corporation being stolen from us. Make your bylaws protective and specific and follow the laws of your state. Contact legal counsel for advice as corporate rules and laws vary from state to state. In the example given the words "team" and "organization" have replaced the corporate name of our organization. You may note the obvious attempts to prevent yet another takeover of this newly formed organization. As my grandmother used to say, an ounce of prevention is worth a pound of cure. Make a takeover of your corporation as difficult as possible. They may scream art you that you are a dictator, but at least you will not lose that organization little Sally and all the other kids on your team have grown to love. So read, evaluate, and contact legal counsel. If you are already involved in an insidious takeover as we were, it may already be too late to stop the ball rolling; and if you have to begin again as we did, I can tell you what we did. It was long. It was involved. You may just want to run away no matter how hard your child pleads with you to stay and fight the good fight. I call myself a recovering volunteer, and I may need a twelve step process before I can claim a path to a cure. Those of us who have been through this just take the recovery one day at a time. It took me a year of pain and stress and toil, but my blood pressure is finally back to normal and I am no longer in danger of having a heart attack or a stroke, according to my doctor.

Banning me from volunteering in the sport has served as a gift, even though it was wrong, and even though it hurt in more ways than one. Remember, people can be cruel; and if you put your faith in people alone, you will always be disappointed.

BYLAWS OF (Insert Corporate Name)
A PUBLIC BENEFIT NONPROFIT CORPORATION

ARTICLE I
NAME

The name of this organization shall be the _____. Herein and after referred to as: (Insert abbreviation of name)

ARTICLE II
OBJECT

The object of this organization shall be to develop, promote, foster and sustain amateur competitive _____ under the auspices of (national organization name if required) This organization shall be the official sponsor of (insert team name). is a charitable organization and is run for a charitable educational purpose and shall not exist for the benefit of only one or two individuals. The (insert team name) will offer (insert sport type) scholarship and event financial assistance as able to families with special needs. The board of directors shall meet at regularly scheduled closed meeting to discuss and determine these and other matters. The Federal Privacy Act will be followed.

ARTICLE III
MEMBERSHIP

Section 1: Membership

Any adult (person over the age of 18) shall be eligible for membership, providing that such adult, or such adult's minor child or children qualify for the sports team. The Head Coach shall establish qualification standards for team swimmers. All members of team may retain membership as long as they remain in good standing. There will be one membership per family. Official voting members must have attached their swimmers to the team through national membership in the parent organization (if required).

Section 2: Application

All applications for membership, together with the national registration fee (if required)and initial dues, shall be given to the head coach who shall notify the Board of Directors and the board will thereafter place the new member on the membership roster, subject to the passing of the probationary membership period of three months). The board of directors reserves the right to review and deny membership of any applicant at any time. The board further reserves the right to remove any member for cause. If membership is denied, the initial dues, if paid, will be refunded. Certain documents must be completed and are mandatory to membership. These will be set forth in the team handbook, and as updated. There shall be a three month probationary period for membership and membership shall not officially commence until the three year time period has passed and until the member is officially accepted into membership by the board of directors after head coach approval.

ARTICLE IV
DUES

Section 1: Authority

The Board of Directors has the responsibility of providing financial viability to the organization, and is so empowered to insure this through establishment of dues and such supplemental fundraising and/or assessments as required. If a member does not desire to participate in fundraising, the board shall determine the average value of that fundraising and the member not desiring to participate in the fundraising will be required to pay the organization. the fair value of that fundraising in which the member does not desire to participate. The member shall be informed in advance of the amount to be required as payment in lieu of the particular fundraising. Requirement to participate in fundraising shall begin with the beginning of the probationary membership period.

Section 2: Payment

Dues are paid monthly. Monthly payments are due on the 1st of the month and are late if not paid by the 10th day of the month. If dues are not submitted by the 10th day of the month and prior arrangements have not been made regarding payment, then the swimmer for whom payment has not been made shall not be allowed to swim until dues are made current.

Section 3: Delinquency

For insurance purposes, the head coach shall be informed on the 10th day of each month as to which families have not paid team dues for that month as that family is no longer in good standing with the organization, unless or until other payment arrangements have been made. The coaches shall not allow a swimmer to swim on the 11th day of that month unless or until payment is made. It shall be the responsibility of the head coach to make sure that the swimmer sits out any session where dues are not paid up to date of payment unless special arrangements have been made with the board of directors. A delinquent family shall have no vote in the organization as that family is not in good standing with the organization by this definition.

Section 4: Inactive Status

A team member who is to be inactive for a period in excess of thirty (30) days may request inactive status and a suspension of dues and remain in good financial standing. This request will be made to the Board of Directors.

Section 4: Exceptions

Exceptions to any of the above can be requested of the Board of Directors. Each request will be decided on its individual merit.

ARTICLE V
TERMINATIONS/SUSPENSIONS

A member or swimmer may be terminated and/or suspended by the Board of Directors when dues are not paid in accordance with the schedule prescribed by the Board of Directors, or by not abiding by the By-Laws and/or rules of the organization.

ARTICLE VI
BOARD OF DIRECTORS & OFFICERS

Section 1: Duties

All matters in the regular coarse of business of the organization shall be managed by its Board of Directors. The responsibility of the board of directors shall be administrative and the making of team policy. The board of directors shall both hire and terminate coaches as they believe in the best interests of the corporation.

Section 2: Number of Directors

The number of Directors shall be five (5). The Board of Directors shall consist of the President, Vice President, Secretary, Treasurer, and Ways and Means Chairperson. The Board of Directors shall be elected by the membership at the October/November meeting held in odd years. In order to serve on the board of directors a member must be in good standing and must have been a member of the organization for a period of no less than one full year. The board of directors is voluntary and no parents of past team members may retain positions on the board. If a child quits or leaves the team, resignation of the parent board member shall immediately ensue, and the remaining board members shall act in appointing a replacement to serve the remainder of the term as set forth herein, where after regular elections shall be held. Vacating of the position of president shall be assumed by the vice president who shall serve out the term of the president.

Section 3: Eligibility

Any member of the organization in good standing has been a member of the organization for a period of no less than one year is eligible to serve on the Board of Directors as stated above. No family shall hold more than one position on the Board at any time. A board member acting in malfeasance or committing any legal crime or wrong shall be immediately dismissed from the board by a majority vote of the remaining board members. Applicable California laws shall apply to the reasonable reliance of any board member as to the representations of another board member, and no board member shall be held liable for acts committed by another or for not acting because of reasonable reliance on representations made by a wrong doing board member.

Section 4: Voting Rights of Board Members

Each member of the Board in attendance shall have one (1) vote. The Head Coach and immediate past President are the 6th and 7th members of the Board with full privileges to participate in the business of the organization, including the right to vote

Section 2: Nomination

Nomination is by a call for volunteers who desire to take office and vote by general membership affirming. No individual may become a board member who has not been a member of the organization for at least one year as stated herein, nor may he be nominated for any position of authority. Prospective and nominated board members must also have exhibited during their membership a willingness to volunteer and to work for the corporation and this willingness must be substantiated by a pattern of volunteering throughout the year prior to nomination. No elections shall be held except as stated herein, and board members may not be elected thr0ough the calling of any special meeting.

Section 3: Term

The Board of Directors shall be elected by ballot to serve for a two (2) year term or until successors are elected, no board member shall serve more than two terms of office on the board in any capacity what-so-ever. The term of office shall begin in May. If there is but one nominee for each office, the ballot may be dispensed with. He founding board shall begin in May with a two year term. The offices of president, secretary and ways and means shall be elected in odd years, and the remaining positions of the board of director shall be elected in even years.

Section 4: Service Limits

No member shall hold more than one office at a time. Each term of office beginning and retroactive from May, shall run for two years and shall expire in May of the second year of office. Should no one come forward to run for the office expiring, and should no one desire to resign from said position, the position may run continuously until time of resignation of that person from that office, excepting that the term may be and run no longer than a total of four years. . It is the hope and desire of the corporation that this shall insure an experienced Board of Directors best able to serve the needs of the corporation.

Section 5: Vacancies

In the event of a vacancy in the office of Vice President, Secretary, Treasurer, or Ways and Means Chairperson, the members of the Board of Directors shall elect a successor to hold office for remainder of the term. In the event of a vacancy in the office of the President, the Vice-President shall assume the duties of the President until a new President can be elected the general membership at the annual meeting. The board of Directors may only be elected as set forth in these bylaws, with no exceptions. Members of the board of directors may only be removed from officer for failure to meet membership criteria, or for behavior constituting malfeasance, or for failure to attend to the duties of the position, and can only be removed by vote of the board of directors, itself; and not by the general membership; excepting that the general membership pay replace the members of the board of directors at the end of the two year term for each respective office, on either odd or even years as specified herein, upon vote and according to these bylaws.

Section 6: Board Meetings

Regular meetings of the Board shall be held each month. Special meetings of the Board may be called upon the request of two (2) members of the Board, or by the board president. Three (3) voting members of the board of directors shall constitute a quorum.

ARTICLE VII
DUTIES OF OFFICERS & BOARD OF DIRECTORS

Section 1: President

The President shall preside at all general meetings of this organization and all meetings of the Board.

Section 2: Vice-President

The Vice-President shall assist the President in all matters, and in the absence of the President shall perform the duties of the President. The Vice-President shall be Chairperson of the Membership Committee.

Section 3: Secretary

The Secretary shall keep records of all the proceedings of the Board and of General Meetings of the membership; shall keep on file all committee reports; shall maintain record books in which the By-Laws, standing rules, policies, and minutes are entered with any amendments to these documents properly reported; shall notify the members of all general meetings; shall prepare correspondence of the Organization.

Section 4: Treasurer

The Treasurer shall receive and disburse the funds for the organization. The Treasurer shall keep all monies of the organization deposited in its name; shall bill members for their dues; shall report all delinquent dues to the Board of Directors; shall make a financial report at meetings of the Board of Directors and of the general membership; shall serve as chairperson of the Budget Committee. No disbursements shall be made without authorization of the Board of Directors

Section 5: Ways and Means

The Ways and Means Chairperson shall be in charge of overall fundraising responsibilities of the organization.

Section 6: Continuity

Each officer, upon the expiration of his/her term of office, shall turn over to his/her successor without delay all records pertaining to the office and other materials belonging to the organization

ARTICLE VIII
ORGANIZATION MEETINGS

Section 1: General Meetings

The regular meetings of the Organization shall be held during the months of April and September, the days to be set by Board of Directors.

A. *<u>April meeting:</u>* The regular meeting in April shall be known as the annual meeting and shall be for the purpose of electing officers on those meetings every two years as election becomes eminent, receiving reports of officers and committees, and any other business that may arise. The newly elected board members shall begin the term of office in the month of May in the year elected. Preparations shall begin for fundraisers and discussions shall take place regarding those fundraisers as well as a call for committee volunteers for those fundraisers.

B. *<u>September Meeting</u>*: The regular meeting in September shall be known as the semi-annual meeting and shall be for the purpose of reviewing the budget of the Organization; reviewing preparations for the short course meet season and hosting of meets, receiving reports of officers and committees, and any other business that may arise.

Section 2: Special Meetings

Special meetings may be called by the President or by the Board of Directors and shall be called upon the request in writing of ten (10) members of the Organization. The purpose of the meetings shall be stated in the call. except in cases of emergency, and then at least ten (10) days notice shall be given. No special, meeting may be called or asked for within 60 (sixty days) of the regularly scheduled bi-annual meetings of the organization. Members of the organization must have attached to the swim team, and be in good standing with all dues paid in full, to call a meeting. The board of directors may grant the request for a special meeting if by majority vote the board of directors believes the call is warranted and prudent and is not contrary to the provisions of these bylaws.

Section 3: Quorums

Fifteen (15) members shall constitute a quorum at a general meeting with one vote per family. No provision shall be made for a proxy vote, or telephonic vote or conference call vote. The President or Vice President must be present at any meeting where a vote is to be taken. The membership shall not control the day-to-day business of the corporation, and it shall have no vote in controlling the day-to-day business of the corporation. The membership may advise the board by taking an advisory vote on matters it desires to be considered by the board of directors at the next regularly scheduled meeting of the board. Only members present who are in good standing are entitled to vote at a general meeting. Each family present shall have one (1) vote. The quorum may not decide organization. policy or dictate administrative duties or direct the coaches in how to coach the swim team in any manner whatsoever, but may vote on other matters and decide as to such things that they desire to have the ***name of corporation*** board evaluate, and the organization board may bring before the quorum such matters as they deem to require general vote. Members are those persons as defined above and herein. The general membership shall have no ability or power to enter into contracts on behalf of the organization, including the hiring or termination of coaches, or to dictate any matters of a contractual nature as this is a part of the day-to-day business of the board.

ARTICLE IX
STANDING COMMITTEES

Section 1: Formation

Standing Committees shall be formed by Board of Directors from time to time as deemed necessary to carry on the work of this Organization. Members shall be appointed by the Board of Directors to serve as Chairpersons of the Standing

Committees. The chairpersons of each committee will solicit members from the membership as required to carry out their charge.

Section 2: Reporting

Chairpersons of standing committees will report in writing to the President of the Board of Directors (or his/her designated representative) on committee activities prior to the 30th day of each month.

Section 3: Continuity

Each chairperson shall endeavor to create a notebook of activities and procedures developed to accomplish his/her charge and, upon the expiration of his/her term, shall turn over to his/her successor without delay all records pertaining to the office and other materials belonging to the organization.

ARTICLE X
PARLIAMENTARY AUTHORITY

The rules contained in the current edition of Robert's Rules of Order, newly revised, shall govern the organization in all cases to which they are applicable and in which they are not inconsistent with these By-Laws and any special rules of order the Organization may adopt. To reflect the state of art technology, any board member may call for a vote by way of email and a majority shall constitute board approval and passage.

ARTICLE XI
BY-LAWS

Section 1: These by laws may be amended as necessary and according to the Laws of the State of California by giving 30 days notice to the general membership in writing and to the board, and must be affirmed by both the general membership and the board with the right of the elected board to veto power of all or part of the amendment(s). These bylaws may not be amended to interfere with the election procedures set forth herein.

ARTICLE XII
DISSOLUTION

Section 1: Procedure

    Should it be necessary to wind up the affairs of this corporation and take the action provided for in Article 7 of the Articles of Incorporation, any officer or member may call a special meeting for this purpose. The person so calling this meeting shall give fourteen (14) days notice of such meeting by mailing said notice to the last known address of each member. There shall be no quorum requirement for a meeting duly called under the provisions of this section.

Section 2: Property

    The property of this organization is irrevocably dedicated to competitive swimming and no part of the net income or assets of this Organization ever inure to the benefit of any private individual. If dissolution, disbandment, inactivation, or other termination of the club is deemed necessary by the general membership, the funds and properties of the club, in excess of the liabilities, shall be distributed to a non-profit fund, foundation or corporation which has established its tax-exempt status under Section 501 (c)-3 of the Internal Revenue Code.

These bylaws shall become effective when adopted/ by a majority of the founding board of directors.

So approved and adopted on _____(date) at _____(time) at_____ (city/state).

Signatures to follow:

Chapter Seventeen

Make Your Coach Contracts Stand For Something!

If you are on the board of directors of a nonprofit organization that "owns" a kids sports team are responsible for the hiring and the firing of coaches because this is a part of the day to day business of the organization for which you are responsible. This means you must act responsibly and investigate everything you may hear about those you have hired, no matter how far fetched an allegation may seem. You have to do this to protect the corporation from liability; and if your corporation is in suspended status, then the liability will fall right onto you as board members, making the responsibility no less than frightening should a serious incident occur. You must always think in terms of Murphy's law and the worst case scenario.

Is there anything you can do to protect yourselves? The answer is yes. Get a rider attached onto your organization's insurance to protect the board of directors from liability. Purchase board of directors' insurance.

While you are at it, checking your insurance that is, make sure that you also have workers compensation insurance, and yes, with everything else that happened to us, there was also no workers compensation insurance as required by law, something that caused several Taco Bell restaurants to be closed in our area and their franchise owner to be criminally charged.

Is there a way around having to do all of this? Yes, you can hire a swim school to supply your coaches and/or hire coaches as independent contractor, making certain these coaches comply with the definition of an independent contractor as that legal definition of what an independent contractor is written in your state.

The main thing is to make your contracts with your coaches clear, and to also follow the letter of the law as to what your requirements are as an employer.

To follow is one example of a contract that has been used with our organization. Note that what is expected of the coach is clearly set forth in the body of the contract. It must be made absolutely clear that the coach is an employee of the board if this is a board owned and run team, and unless you are hiring an independent contractor where the coach is free to make certain decisions on his own, you are responsible, the buck stops with the organization, and the coach is expected to adhere to the terms of the contract. If this is a problem, ask the coach to leave because with0ut a measure of control, your organization has nothing but trouble ahead. If you have done things right you have an at will contract, so you can say good-bye without cause, unless at will contracts are prohibited in your state, in which case you will have to build your case against the coaches.

In any event it is always better to be reasonable and not to terminate a coach unless you have cause, and even if you have cause you can still expect some fall out from those who are either willing to forgive, whose children were not involved and/or put in danger, or who just don't care if the coach is a child molester because their children are either the incorrect or sex preferred by the child molester, or their children will surely say no, or there must have been some kind of consent because the coach is really a great guy and the team is doing well and winning lots of medals, trophies and ribbons.

To follow is a sample coach's contract, but the main thing to remember is that you need to put everything you want that coach to do into your contract, and the coach you hire needs to know that you (the board of directors of the corporation), are his boss, just like any other boss at any other job. Your coach will need to let the board know when he will not be present, so that his position can either be covered or the game or practice cancelled. If your coach will be unable to meet his obligations and have to miss a game or practice, he should be prepared to explain why, and he should have a good reason for not being there because there are children affected by his absence; and our children are not only the innocent among us, they are also our future's most precious commodity..

Employment Contract Between (*Name of Coach*) and (*Name of Corporation*), a Nonprofit Corporation

The (*Name of Corporation*), a nonprofit corporation, (*hereinafter referred to as: abbreviation of corporation name*), and (*name of coach*), an individual, hereby enter into the following fully binding month to month contract for employment for good and valuable consideration from both parties to this contract.

(*Name of Corporation*) agrees to pay (name of coach) the sum of (*amount of money*) for his services as (*position*), and (*name of coach*) agrees to perform the following duties:

1. (*Name of Coach*) shall coach that certain group of beginning swimmers on the team commonly known as "the age groupers" for two hours per week;

2. (*Name of coach*) shall coach that certain group on the team commonly known as "the Juniors" for approximately one and one half to two hours per day, depending on level of ability and need as determined by (*name o coach*), Monday through Friday consecutively. There may be a cross training activity or other team entertainment activity scheduled Saturdays as determined necessary by (*name of coach and name of corporation*), except on those Saturdays when there is a swim meet or as otherwise approved by the Board of Directors of (*name of corporation*).

3. (*Name of coach*) shall attend each and every (*meet, game*) on each and every day said (meet, game) that is offered by (the local sports governing organization), where the Junior group may participate, or the age group may participate, unless excused from attendance by the Board of Directors of (*name of corporation*);

4. The amount of payment herein referenced to includes and is inclusive of preparation time, for which there shall be no additional pay;

5. The Head Coach, whoever that shall be, shall meet and confer with (*name of coach under this contract*), and (*coach name*) shall make himself available for such a meeting no less than once a week, excepting that (*name of coach*) shall not be made accountable for such a meeting should the Head Coach not make him or herself available for such a meeting;

6. It is further understood that (*name of coach*) shall maintain all insurance and coaches cards and credentials as needed and required of this position and shall attend the local governing sports organization meetings, if specially requested by the Board of Directors of (*name of corporation*) and make a report on the same to the Board of Directors of (*name of corporation*), if so requested;

7. Christmas Day and Christmas Eve shall be paid holidays, and Thanksgiving and the Friday thereafter shall be paid holidays;

8. (*Name of coach*) is an employee of (*name of corporation*) and will and agrees to follow and enforce all the rules set forth in the team handbook and all other rules of the (*name of city*), and (*name of state*) and all federal rules and regulati9ns as well as the rules and regulations of the governing sport at both the local and national levels;

9. Children shall be properly supervised by (*name of coach*) at all times, and (*name of coach*) shall follow the line of sight rule, making certain the children are always supervised and within the line of sight of the coach, unless the children are leaving the area to go to the restroom, and then the coach shall make sure the children are supervised by a responsible adult of the same sex as the child (or children) using the bathroom facilities;

10. Breaking of any of the provisions set forth herein by (*name of coach*) shall constitute a breach of this contract;

11. Disrespect of the board of directors of (*name of corporation*) shall constitute an immediate breach of this contract.

12. After period one year there shall be a one week paid vacation that must coincide with the off season of (*the sport*) year's schedule..

This is a contract at will. This contract shall run from month to month, automatically renewed without notice, and each party reserves the right to cancel this contract of employment without any cause what-so-ever.

This is the total and complete and binding agreement by and between the parties and may be modified only in writing and by full approval of the Board of Directors of *(name of corporation)*.and by a majority vote of said board, and agreed upon also in writing by and through the signature of (*name of coach*).

.

Parties sign and date document.

Chapter Eighteen

The Immigration Reform and Control Act, Form I-9

The Immigration Reform and Control Act, Form I-9 must be filled out, signed by the employee, and then signed by an officer of the corporation, preferably the president of the corporation. The employee must show proof he is in the United States of America legally and is entitled to work. This means the employee must either have a green card or be a citizen of the United States of America. The form must be filled out and the proof given within three days of the beginning of employment, or the corporation may be fined for breaking immigration laws. Every employee must comply with this requirement. This is not based on either race or nationality.

In our case, this took nearly a month; and guess who was finally shown the documents and who signed the I-9 forms? It was not the board president as the boar of directors of our corporation required, nor was it the pro-bono counsel of record. You guessed it, it was the illustrious embezzling treasurer seeking coalition with the newly hired coaches to whom she bad mouthed the other members of the board, and against whom she was later to conspire to take over the corporation in order to protect her scam and what she had been doing for the last four years. You see this board of directors of four months had begun to ask questions such as where is this paper and where is that paper and why is there no record of the head coach's employment with the IRS? It was now up to her to go to these newly hired coachers and the parents brought with them to the team and to begin a pattern of action to discredit them, complaining behind their backs about everything they did and about every decision made by them on behalf of the corporation, no matter how small the decision was, so this is exactly what she did. She was beloved. She was trusted. She was a con artist. It was very easy to do.

You can find the form by going to the US Citizen and Immigration Services website at http://uscis.gov/graphics/howdoi/faqeev.htm and then by reading what they have to say and clicking on the sidebar where the term "Immigration forms" is listed and follow the way to get to form I-9. If you want to go directly to the I-9 Form then just go to the following web address: http://uscis.gov/graphics/formsfee/forms/files/i-9.pdf. .

The US Citizen and Immigration Services information website states: "The Immigration Reform and Control Act made all U.S. employers responsible to verify the employment eligibility and identity of all employees hired to work in the United States after November 6, 1986. To implement the law, employers are required to complete Employment Eligibility Verification forms (Form I-9) for all employees, including U.S.

citizens." It explains that the employer must obtain and retain an I-9 form on every new employee unless the employee was hired before November 7, 1986, and the employee has been continuously employed by the same employer." It also explains: ***Form I-9 need not be completed for individuals***: It those individuals provide domestic services in a private household or in a home that are not regular and are only occasional services not performed on a regular basis (something that should not apply to your organization at all); ***Or for those individuals:***: Who work for the employer as an independent contractor (i.e. carry on independent business, contract to do a piece of work according to their own means and methods, without specific direction as to how and when work should be done, and are subject to control only as to results. The employer cannot tell the employee when to work and the only requirement of the employee is that the work is done. The employer does not set work hours or provide necessary tools to do the job. The employer does not have authority to hire and fire those working for the independent contractor.

See: http://uscis.gov/graphics/howdoi/faqeev.htm for further details and specifics of the law as it applies to independent contractors.

Hiring an independent contractor may work for your organization as it later worked for us as an intermediate measure, providing the independent contractor you hire is serious about your sport and has the same common goals long term your organization has, and providing your organization is willing to give up control. Simply set up a contract with the independent contractor stating your terms.

Is Requiring the I-9 Form Discriminatory?

As stated above, the law and this requirement is not discriminatory in nature as it is required of every new employee, and if an employee has a problem with this requirement of law, as the new employees of our corporation did, then perhaps you should reconsider hiring them as employees of your corporation. On the other hand, if you are hiring an independent contractor as defined by your state and as defined above, you may dispense with the I-9 form, because in actuality you are hiring an entity responsible for itself. Do not allow yourself to be bullied into not following the letter of the law, and do not feel guilty for requiring the latter of the law be followed. Some people think they can make their own rules, and even if they get away with it, it does not make the doing of a wrong thing right. When a tree falls in the forest, just because no one sees it fall, or hears it fall, does not mean the tree has not fallen. Use the I-9 form faithfully and because this form may change from year to year, always make sure you are using a current I-9 form; and always make certain you are in compliance with this law. If your employees refuse compliance in filling of this form and in presenting their identification documents to you, tell them to go and find another job and to stop darkening your door. Normal employees who are legally in the United States will have no problem with complying with this government requirement. Laws change from time to time so always keep up to date as to what is required of your corporation as an employer. It is true that ignorance of the law is no excuse for not following the law, even though many may claim otherwise, and if you do not know the law or want to find out what the law as to your corporation is and comply with it, then please do not volunteer. You will only get yourself into trouble. Be informed, be aware and beware because just like in the old time story of little orphan Annie, "The boogie man will get you if you don't watch out!" The boogie man got us, and our eyes were wide opened!

Chapter Nineteen
The Letter of Termination

Even though you have hired your employees at will, providing you are in a state that slows at will employment, you will still want to present your coaches with termination notices or letters in order to best preserve a paper trail as to why the coach or coaches were terminated. In our instance, the coaches refused to accept their letters of termination because they stated they were "advised" not to accept them, presumably by some legal counsel, perhaps even the counsel hired by the terminated treasurer who was creating an artifice, fraud, scheme and design to prttect herself and take over our corporation and team. The coaches were handed the letters, each in turn, and let them fall to the ground. The good guys board then emailed the notices of termination and verbally told the coaches they were terminated.

The reaction was one of belligerent hostility and a refusal to accept the termination of employment, even though two of the coaches were still in their ninety day probationary period.

These coaches had been forewarned by. the embezzling treasurer of their fates, and were prepared to act accordingly, even though two of them had no valid coaching credentials and were therefore for all intents and purposes not only in immediate breach of contract, (although that fact was at that time unknown to the board of directors), but they were also committing a fraud against the corporation by holding themselves out as qualified and credentialed coaches.

In the long run the local and national sports committees refused to address this issue as well, with the local committee board of review stating it would not interfere with employee/employer relationships, while at the same time they turned over the organization that was ours to them. Again, this was done by a local governing sports organization that was also in suspension and perhaps could not bear as the pot to call the kettle black

Nevertheless, if it is your intention to terminate a coach that should never have been hired in the first place, or to terminate a coach who is in breach of contract or has done some wrong the corporation's board of directors believes is intolerable. To follow is one example of a document you can use. You will need to make your letter fact specific to your case and use language in your letter that leads back to your coach contract and its contents, if applicable. Please note laws vary from state to state and your circumstances are unique, so please do not accept this as specific legal advice of any kind. For specific advice on any area of the law, please consult your own attorney.

Your reasons for termination of your coach will be specific. Be as specific as your reasons in your letter of termination. Also remember that you may encounter opposition to you actions no matter how valid, sensible and necessary they are. While our letter of termination gave no doubt as to the reasons our board had for termination of our coaches, our local sports committee would not consider the wrongs committed by these coaches when we were challenged by our embezzling treasurer and her attorneys who like snakes in the grass, hid behind these coaches and those who wanted only to take our team and all we had.. We were faced with the good old boy syndrome, and we were not one of the good old boys; however, our terminated treasurer was. Even though she had committed a grievous wrong, and even though these coaches had endangered our children, no one would listen to a single word we said, even at the national level, with the national level refusing to address any issues not addressed at the local level hearing, and the local level refusing to listen to anything we had to say, choosing instead to accept as true misstatements of the truth and a skewing of the facts to meet their own selfish needs. It was supposed to be about the children, but it was not about the children or about doing what was best for the children. It was about greed, power and self-preservation of adults and a social hierarchy and power base for some unknown, bewildering and undiscovered reason, and some of these adults were getting away with the commission of extremely serious wrongs. It was not a good example for the children.

They all hid behind a veil of jurisdiction, but the problem was the veil was sheer and you could see right through it. It wasn't anyone's problem, and no one would take any responsibility on any level to exercise the powers they had in favor of right.

Written on corporate letterhead

(Date)

Dear (name of terminated employee),

The (name of corporation) Board of Directors has voted to terminate your employment, effective (insert date and time). The primary reason for your termination is child endangerment. On two separate occasions the (name of corporation) coaches individually as well as in concert with one another allowed children to remain alone on the Naval Amphibious base in breach of their contracts as well as in breach of agreements between themselves, ourselves, and the City of (name city), and in violation of the memorandum of understanding between the Navy and all applicable parties requiring a (name of corporation) employed coach be with the children at all times while the children are on the base. On the first occasion of this breach you were notified of its seriousness, and a promise was given that it would not happen again, yet each of you allowed it to happen a second time. While you may consider the time the children were alone insignificant, the board of directors does not. The children should never be left alone on base, or anywhere else. Children are a precious resource. This is a very serious situation for us all, and the board has made this decision only after great thought and deliberation and with much concern for the continuity of coaching for the children. You were hired as part of a coaching team; therefore the board has decided to terminate you as a coaching team.

Other reasons for your termination include, but are not limited to the following reasons: 1) Your contract states you must attend each and every swim meet and each of every day of any and all local meets in which a swimmer of yours attends. You have failed to do this and/or to cause at least one meet not to be covered; and you recently announced you would be out of town for another swim meet , refusing to defer permission to the board of directors of (name of corporation); 2) You have failed to assure the children have a deck chaperone on deck each and every day hidden swim as directed by the board; 3) You have not assured all required paperwork has been turned in causing consternation to the board and possible voiding of insurance; 4) You have not shown up for practice on at least two occasions and did not get prior clearance from the board as required in your contract; 5) the I-9 form required by the IRS and others and supporting documents were not presented to the board president, or to the pro bono counsel in a timely fashion, and as directed, but presented to another; 6) You have been allowing individuals without required paperwork to swim, etc.

The board feels you are not a good match for (corporation name), and that your services will be better appreciated elsewhere. (Corporation name) is a family oriented group dedicated to children. Because you apparently feel you may skip practices and/or schedule practices at your will without notifying the board, and others, this contributes to the aforementioned problems. It is the belief of the board that your skills will be better appreciated in another setting. We wish you the best of luck.

Sincerely,

(Insert name), President of (name of corporation)
On behalf of the Board of Directors of (name of corporation)

Chapter Twenty
Letters of Tax Exempt Status

    Sometimes you will need to have letters from the federal government attesting to tax exempt status, even if you don't need them because you are exempt from the requirement because your organization may be receiving donations and income from those who want proof you are actually tax exempt. You need to request letters of tax exemption within fifteen months of the incorporation of your organization, and if you miss the deadline, you will not get the letters of exemption. This does not mean you are not tax exempt, it just means you will not have any way to prove you are tax exempt. There is a form you must fill out, sign and mail within the proscribed time frame and an application .fee. Although the amount of the required filing fee may change, at the time of the writing of this handbook the fee was set at $500.00 for nonprofit corporations making an average of $25,000.00 over a three year period, and $150.00 for those corporations making less than an average of $25,000,00 over a three year period.

In order to be tax-exempt as an organization under Internal Revenue Code Section 501(c)(3) of the Code, the organization must be organized and operated exclusively for one or more of the purposes set forth in the Internal Revenue Code. Most importantly, none of the earnings of the organization may inure to any private shareholder or individual. You cannot participate in anything political as well, but the main problem with being tax exempt as a sports organization is that you cannot exist solely for the purpose of paying a coach where all you do is pay one person or two because then the earnings of the organization would inure to the benefit of one or two Individuals and your tax exempt status could be challenged. Therefore, you should offer sports scholarships and the like, educate the public about the advantages of your sport and do other charitable acts that apply to your organization. Basically a Section 501 (c) (3) organizations is a charitable organization, so this is how you must conduct yourself to qualify as being "charitable" If you are a charitable organization that qualifies under the Internal Revenue Code Section referenced above, then you will be eligible to receive tax deductible contributions. This does not mean team dues are tax deductible, because when members pay team dues, they are paying for a service, the service of coaching. To structure your dues payments as if you are offering an income tax deduction, by declaration or implication, may increase your participant numbers, but you will also be committing a fraud on the IRS. For more information you should consult IRS Form 557.

What Is a Tax Exempt Purpose According to the IRS?

The exempt purposes set forth in IRC Section 501 (c)(3) are as follows: charitable, religious, educational, scientific, literary, testing for public safety, fostering national or international amateur sports competition, and the prevention of cruelty to children or animals. The term charitable may mean many things. It may mean the acts performed by the organization give relief to the poor, the distressed, or the underprivileged. The charitable purpose may be for the advancement of religion or for the advancement of education or for the advancement of science. A charitable purpose could involve the building or maintenance of a public building, or a monument, or maintenance of public works. A charitable purpose may be geared towards the elimination of prejudice or discrimination. It may advocate defense of human and civil rights .

These are only some of the qualifying categories, but you get the idea. You have to do something other than just hire a coach, so think about it carefully. To be organized exclusively for a charitable purpose, the organization must also be a corporation, community chest, fund, or foundation. A charitable trust is also a fund or foundation and will qualify. However, an individual will not qualify as a tax exempt organization. .

The articles of organization or of incorporation must limit the organization's purposes to one or more of the exempt purposes stated in Internal Revenue Code Section 501 (c) (3), so read it carefully before you proceed. Then adopt the code language into your articles of incorporation.

The purposes stated in the articles of organization should also be limited by reference to Internal Revenue Code Section 501 (c)(3). The assets of the organization must be permanently dedicated to an exempt purpose. This means if the organization dissolves, whether voluntarily or involuntarily, its remaining assets must be distributed for an exempt purpose or turned over to the federal government or to the state or to the local government for a public purpose. The articles of organization should have in it a clause stating that if the organization is dissolved the assets will be distributed to an organization, as stated above, for an exempt purpose. Your Application for tax exemption will be approved more quickly if this provision is included in the articles of incorporation. You also need to attach your articles of incorporation to the application for the exemption. In our set of circumstances we had no assets as everything in our bank account was literally owned by the state and federal governments as it was money withheld from paychecks in scared trust and not properly forwarded under law. So when the board of directors determined the organization was insolvent and would more than likely have to liquidate because there were no assets except for that money withheld from paychecks and not forwarded to the governmental entities (and there were still significant funds missing beyond that which was in the bank account), the powers that be determined in their grand sense of foolishness, that the board who was comprised of the good guys merely wanted to liquidate the corporation to steal the funds for the new corporation formed with knowledge of the State of California Employee Development Department to keep the kids in water, and with the promise that all the funds would be put in trust with them for the benefit of governmental and other creditors. They refused to even call the state to determine what we said was true, and refused to believe we were only trying to place these so called assets with the rightful owners of those assets, the state of California and the Internal Revenue Service of the United States of America. The result was the assets were actually stolen from the state and federal governments with not only the blessings of the powers that be, but also with their help and assistance, and this continued right up the ladder to the top, with no one bothering to make a single phone call to determine if what we said about anything was true even though we supplied both names and phone numbers to prove what we said was the absolute truth .

The point is if you have assets, which we did not, they must be dedicated to a charitable purpose at all times, even when you dissolve and cease to exist. Anything left over must be redirected to a charitable purpose unless you want to lose your charitable status creating a retrospective legal mess. Also, if you think you have assets and you do not, then you need to do everything in your power to see to it the assets get to where they belong, because if you don't .then you simply become a part of the problem, not a part of the solution. You become a co-conspirator rather than whistleblower. As for me? I would rather do what is right and just and act according to the law. Give me the whistle and I will either blow it, or I will advise those I represent to blow hard. My mother always said two wrongs do not make a right, and she is one of the wisest people I know. My way of practicing law is to advise my clients to take responsibility for their wrongs, and if my clients don't agree with that, then they can seek new counsel. I am known as the tar and feather attorney because I do not tolerate anything less than the letter of the law, and when even an attorney is not doing something right, I will let him know and if he chooses to proceed in an incorrect manner, then I will bring the matter before the judge and let the judge decide. My credo is no one is perfect, except for God, and everyone makes mistakes, but it is absolutely necessary to admit your mistakes and to take responsibility for them. Unfortunately, the rest of the world does not often see things my way, and even if they are with sin, they will cast their stones, often against the pure of heart because they cannot tolerate looking into a mirror that reflects what they are not and what they would really and truly like to be!!.

Please refer to Chapter Fifteen of this handbook for
an example of California articles of incorporation. In your state these may be referred to as articles of organization or some other term, and what your particular state may require may differ from state of California requirements, so again remember that laws vary from state to state, and for specific advise on any area of the law you should contact an attorney licensed to do business in the state in which you reside. These articles are sufficient, when filed in the state of California to qualify your organization as tax exempt, and to be submitted and attached to your 1023 Form, and for additional information you may need or to answer further questions?
http://www.irs.gov/charities/article/0,,id=96109,00.html   :

Chapter Twenty-One

Your Application for Membership

You need to have an application for membership, not because the state or federal government requires it of you, but just because it makes good sense. Our application at least protected us during the probationary period of three months. Those one of the newly hired coaches brought with him who intended to take over the team, (and ultimately did), felt insulted by the probationary period and let us know immediately. Other normal people without ulterior motives had no problem with the application. So if you find that a large or substantial number of individuals all want to join your team at once, and they object to a probationary period, you might want to think about what their possible motives might be. Of course we saw this red flag; and when we were told that they had a plan the first time they could not get there way and be on the military base because of the code orange and the military's memorandum of understanding between the team and the city, we sensed and pretty much knew a battle was coming. However, we fooled ourselves into believing we could just get these people to like us and what we had to offer as a team. What we did not know was the coach they came with came from a place where no one was too happy with them or the coach and when they came, the door had pretty much been shut as to the possibility of future return. Apparently they and the coach were known trouble makers, and it appeared that only one board member of the good guys had seen through all of this, and she could not get the rest to listen when she said, "Get rid of them. They are trouble. They have no respect for anything." Of course, I was not on the board of directors and had no say. I was legal counsel and advisor and that was all.

They wanted what we had, and when the treasurer's wrongdoing was discovered, and she was terminated from the board of directors for this serious wrong, coincidentally discovered about the same time these coaches caused children to be left alone on a military base during a code orange for the second time causing their termination for endangering the children, among other reasons too numerous to mention, this created the perfect impetus to put the plan of the bad guys into action, while the treasurer was given the opportunity to hide behind the terminated coaches. The bottom line was if the good guys board could be removed, then the good guys could not turn the treasurer over to the authorities, because they would have no legal standing to report her at all because they would no longer be on the board of directors of the team.

So the end result was the bad guys took over the team and the bank account of the team by the terminated treasurer hiring attorneys who orchestrated the matter. The end result was not only the taking of the team, but the taking of funds that did not belong to the team, but were assets held in trust, money taken from paychecks of the employees of the team as withholding of taxes, etc.

As unbelievable as it all sounds, all of this and more is true. So what you need to do is protect yourselves. Give no one the benefit of any doubt. If someone is not a good fit for your team, invite them to immediately leave. It will be less difficult for you to do this, than it will be for you to fight in order to keep your team and its nonprofit organization, and it will also be far less costly in terms of time and attorneys fees, especially if you don't have a free attorney like me who is willing to stick out her neck for the sake of charity and the children.

Most good attorneys enjoy a legal fight based on an intellectual argument about the law, but they do not enjoy mudslinging, stupidity, arrogance and playing the good old boy game. The more specific you can make your documents, the easier will be the task of the attorney to preserve your organization, so leave nothing to doubt, and leave nothing to mere chance. Think of the worst case scenario when preparing your documents and do not worry about offending anyone, because unless they intend to do the crime, they will sign.

To follow is our membership application. You application should be specific to you needs and define exactly what you expect from someone becoming a part of you team and join your organization. You should be strong about this and not waiver. If you waiver as the good guys did, you may end up just as we ended up, and that is fighting to do the right thing against all odds, with your only satisfaction being that you tried to do the right thing, and your only mistake being you did not act swiftly enough at any step of the way, even though you acted as quickly as you could, because after all, you do have a life, a job, a home and a family, and board meetings are only once a month. You need to keep hold of your organization, get rid of the riff raff and if you find an embezzler, no matter how much you want to help this person do the right thing, turn the matter over to the police while you still have a chance. Erring on the side of caution may lead you out into the cold dark night of a cruel reality, and reality is not always fun. In fact, in reality the truth of what is and has been can be downright terrifying, not to mention mind sobering. I know you want to believe the best of everyone, especially if that everyone is someone you thought was doing all this good, but this is why Jeffrey Dahmer got away with mass murder. No one believed nice looking guy like him would do it either.

So when it comes to right and wrong, the best idea is to face the wrong head on and resolve the wrong before the wrong overtakes the right. God helps those who help themselves. Don't sit around and expect to have God do everything for you while you sit idly by and watch the sins of the world.

Everything You Never Wanted To Know About Your Nonprofit Corporation

Application for Membership in *Name of Organization*, a Nonprofit Corporation

Completion of form is mandatory

This is an application for membership in *Name of Organization.* a charitable organization organized for educational purposes and for the benefit of children and the community at large. *Name of Organization* offers a competition level swim program and hosts the *name of major fundraiser* in its endeavors to serve the community at large. It may be that your child has been swimming with *Name of Organization* for a week or so, and now it is time to decide if you will make a commitment to join. In order to be accepted as a member of *Name of Organization* you must complete the New Membership Packet. This application is only one of the papers that you must complete in order to become a member of *Name of Organization*. This is something like an application for a job. The completion of this document and its signing will be followed by a probation period of three months. You will be a member of *Name of Organization*, but you will be a probationary member, you will be a member of the general membership when the probationary period has passed. This time will give you a chance to determine if you are happy with our program and will give us an opportunity to determine if you and your child are right for our program. During this period of time, or during any period of time for which you are a member of *Name of Organization*, any deviation from or breaking any of the rules set forth in the documents herein, as to the Honor Code, The Terms and Conditions of Participation, or any rules set forth by the *Name of Organization* Military Base , or the City of _____ with regard to the *Name of Organization* use of the Military pool facilities will cause *Name of Organization* to refuse your application for membership. During this time or during any other time of your membership, any failure to follow the rules of *Name of Organization*, the Military or the City of _____, whether set forth in the attached documents or not, will cause you

Everything You Never Wanted To Know About Your Nonprofit Corporation

to be expelled from ***Name of Organization*** and any use of the NAB facility. We Welcome you to ***Name of Organization*** and hope you will be happy and satisfied with our program.

Parent(s) names_____

Name of child(ren)_____

Address of parent(s)_____

Address of child(ren)_____

Phone number(s) _____

Email address_____

Please sign and date this application and return with all required documents to your child's coach to begin the application process.
We, the undersigned family of _____(names of children) hereby make application for membership in ***Name of Organization*** and agree to abide by all the rules, terms and conditions of ***Name of Organization***, and _____ (name of pool or city).

Signed_____
Dated:_____

Chapter Twenty-Two

**They Want the Rules, So Give Them the Rules,
Or Just Let Them Eat Cake!**

Everybody wants the rules, so you should give them the organization and team rules. However, even if everybody says they want the rules, do not expect them to be happy with the rules you give them. Sometimes the rules have been there for a long time and everyone has followed the rules without question and so you think there is no need to put the rules in writing, and you think that even if you put the rules in writing it is really no big deal because the rules are the rules , and rules are made to be followed, not broken. You figure it is like the law, something to be adhered to without question, and so you think the rules and the writing of them are no big deal. What you don't realize is that those newcomers to you team may not like the rules, even if they begin as guests on your team. For them the rules are there to be broken and then changed, exactly in that order. They need to see the rules in order to change them.

This is why our newcomers asked to see the rules and the bylaws of our organization. They wanted to come in and take over and change them, and nothing would stop them. All they had to do was make it so that there were more of them than there was of us, or to simply declare that those who were us no longer were members of the organization. It was simple. It was a plan, It was their plan.

When they were given the rules and the application for membership and saw everything we were and what we stood for, they did not want to be a part of us, they wanted to steal what we had, and so they just stole what we had!.

Make your rules. Stick with your rules. Those who intend to abide by your rules will have no complaints about them. Those who seek to break the rules will complain. Immediately suggest to them that they are not a good fit for your organization and invite them off the team, or before you know it, they won't be inviting you to leave, they will be telling you to leave. Stress that probationary period and give no ground.

If they have to wait a year to take over a board of directors, or more because you have staggered terms of office set forth in your bylaws, they will get the idea you are serious about what you have and will either comply or leave. See Chapter Sixteen of this handbook to discover what we did to make our new bylaws, (those created for our second corporation created to keep the kids in water while we sought to regain our organization, revive its corporate status and get the bank funds to the rightful owners of those funds), clearer and more protective of this organization than were the bylaws of our first organization. Fool me once, shame on you. Fool me twice, shame on me.

To follow are the rules and regulations we set forth in writing upon the request of those members who came to our team with one of the new coaches hired by the good guys who had to be terminated because he did not show up for work, without giving excuse, and caused children, specifically a group of about six teenage girls, to be left alone on a military base during a national code orange alert, endangering their well being.

Of course, the excuse was one of the young girls was "almost eighteen", but the good guys said that didn't count, the coach must follow the rules and the almost eighteen child who has just turned seventeen a year later was not hired by the board, was not a certified coach, and the lack of the presence of a coach further voided all insurance, especially troubling to this board when they later discovered there was no protective corporate veil and had something happened, the onus of responsibility would have flowed down to each of them personally.

By the way, the good guys were right. It doesn't take a rocket scientist or even a lawyer to figure out that you do not leave attractive teenage girls wearing nothing but swimsuits and towels alone at night on a military base filled with strong, young, handsome alpha males roaming about freely, especially when they are left sitting near a men's locker room next to a men's gym. It was a bad situation just waiting to happen, and the good guys are just grateful it didn't happen!

To top everything off, because we were so nice, when we gave them the rules, we welcomed the newcomers to our team with a party and a cake, not to mention Tootsie Pop Tuesdays and "To De-Vine Thursdays (complete with red licorice vines) for the kids!

Everything You Never Wanted To Know About Your Nonprofit Corporation

RULES, TERMS AND CONDITIONS FOR PARTICIPATION
Name of Corporation
(A Nonprofit Corporation)

1. The yearly USA Swimming registration fee is not refundable and must be paid prior to the swimmer entering the water. New swimmers may participate for a maximum of one day prior to payment of the registration fees.

2. When a swimmer is moved from one group to another, he/she must pay the monthly fee for the highest group in which they participate.

3. MONTHLY DUES ARE TO BE PAID BY THE FIRST (1ST) DAY OF THE MONTH AND SHALL BE CONSIDERED DELINQUENT AND LATE BY THE 15th DAY OF THE MONTH. NONPAYMENT OF MONTHLY DUES PAST THE TEN DAY GRACE PERIODS, WHICH IS THE 15th DAY OF THE MONTH, WILL NECESSITATE NON-PARTICIPATION FOR THE SWIMMER(S) UNTIL PAYMENT IS MADE. A late fee of 10% will be assessed after the 15th of the month. Members whose accounts are not paid in full by the end of the month will not be allowed to swim. A swimmer who is inactive for a period of 30 days may request inactive status and a suspension of dues and may remain in good standing. All requests must be made in writing. Swimmers who dues are not paid in full within 30 days of the due date, including penalties, will be required to pay a reinstatement fee of ½ (one half)

month's dues to reactivate any account delinquent or inactive for 30 days. Exceptions can be made on a case by case basis and by written confidential application to the board.

4. Meet entry fees are in addition to the monthly dues. Nonpayment of entry fees will also necessitate non-participation for the swimmer(s) in that meet.

5. Should a swimmer decide to discontinue participation in the program with ***Name of Organization***, the monthly dues for the month of which he/she swims any portion thereof and any outstanding entry fees are considered an obligation to ***Name of Organization***, and are payable upon termination of participation. Nonpayment of any such dues due will be reported to the ***name of local sport's governing body***.

6. All swimmers, who are members of ***Name of Organization***, are required to participate at their highest level of achievement in championship meets (including relays).

7. Each family is responsible for volunteering at all hosted swim meets or shall be fined $20 for non participation as a volunteer. Each family shall pay a $15 snack bar fee for any and all meets hosted unless notified otherwise.

8. Each parent and swimmer is responsible for reading and understanding the contents of the "***Name of Corporation*** Handbook"

9. Each team swimmer will be asked to sign a swimmer "Code of Conduct". Failure to comply with this code may result in the swimmer being asked to leave the team.

10. Each swimmer shall sign a team commitment form. Fair share dues may be assessed according to the bylaws of **_Name of Corporation_** under fundraising requirements.

REGARDING THE MILITARY BASE, HERINAFTER REFERRED TO AS THE "BASE"

11. No parent who is not carrying military ID shall enter the base with or without cause so long as the base has a restricted access rule, except as follows: two deck chaperones to assist with taking the swimmers to the restrooms and with other needs. No parent shall fail to follow any rule or rules set forth by the base or by the City of _____ whether or not such rule is set forth herein.

12. The parent shall explain to their swimmer(s) that no child shall be allowed to leave the deck without chaperone or lifeguard escort for any reason whatsoever. Swimmers may not use the locker room area for changing and must use the bathroom before 7:00 PM, except in dire emergency, and then only accompanied by deck chaperone or lifeguard.

13. If a swimmer is told not to come to practice because a requirement of payment has not been met, then it shall be expected that the swimmer will sit out the swim session and wait to be driven back to the carpool pick-up drop off point. Parents are informed that on the 11th day of each month or shortly thereafter the coach(s) will be informed and given a list as to which accounts are in arrears and those swimmers will be asked to sit out the session until transported back to the pick up point at the end of the session. Those families with sudden financial hardship are encouraged to inquire of the board to make arrangements for other payment options. If parents are aware they have not paid dues as of the 10th day of the month, they should not send their child to practice. Parents will be responsible for those ten days at a pro-rata rate if the family decides not to return to ***Name of Corporation*** and all out standing balances shall be reported to the ***Name of local governing organization*** in accordance with USA swimming procedure(s) and current rules and/or ***Name of Corporation*** practice(s).

14. All parents shall be at the pick-up drop off point at least ten minutes prior to the expected arrival of their children at the finish time of their children's practice session. No parent is allowed on deck except for the deck chaperone and one assistant and those persons specially approved by the board of directors for good cause. Parents with military ID are excluded as they transport their children and other children on and off the base and therefore must have deck entry.

15. Parents shall explain all rules to their children and shall expect all rules to be followed. Parents shall explain to their children that there shall be no deck changing on deck and that children should wear their suits under warm coverings easily removed and quickly put back on over wet swimsuit in order to quickly vacate the deck at the finish of final practice, and that no child shall be allowed to leave the deck without a ride to the drop off point.

16. Parents who are drivers on to and off of the NAB shall come to the deck to pick up the children, and those they are transporting to the pick-up drop off point, and shall not require children to leave the deck to find their drivers, as no child will be allowed to leave the deck unescorted.

17. This is a team and team is not spelled with the letter "I", therefore parents are strongly encouraged, if they have base access, and space in their cars, and military privileges, to stop by the pick up point and inquire if any swimmer or chaperone is in need of a ride on to the base.

18. No parent shall approach or otherwise direct or interfere with the coaching of their children when they are on deck, whether or not that parent has military access, unless solicited by and requested by the child's coach to do so. All parents shall remain at the seating area of the deck and shall not approach the pool unless and/or until directed to do so by one or more of the coach(s).

19. The directives of the head deck chaperone are to be followed for the safety and well being of all **_Name of Corporation_** swimmers. This document consists of the essence of the directives and rules of **_Name of Corporation_**. These rules may be altered or modified at any time without notice. However, each parent shall be informed by email and/or posting on the **_Name of Corporation_** website; **_insert web address_** of any changes in the rules set forth above, and once notice is given either constructive or actual to the parents of **_Name of Corporation_** swimmers, continuation in the **_Name of Corporation_** swim program is acquiescence and acceptance of those additional rules and or regulations and shall become a binding part of this agreement.

20. All swimmers shall turn in Military Tank (pool) releases, all medical forms and releases and information sheets and any other materials, papers or documents and things, deemed necessary by the **_Name of Corporation_** board as a condition of swimming with **_Name of Corporation_**, and failure to submit these materials to the coach or deck chaperone in a timely fashion will result in the swimmer not being able to swim and requiring them to sit out each swim session until full compliance is made with all requests for such materials. The coach will receive a directive from the board of directors as to which families are in violation of this directive and shall enforce the aforementioned rule vigorously.

21. Any ambiguities in any of the above provisions numbered 1-21, and in the below provisions 22-32 shall be decided in favor of the board of directors of **_Name of Corporation._**. Any questions regarding any

ambiguities in the above should be asked of and answered by the ***Name of Corporation*** board and/or its legal representative in writing prior to the signing of this agreement, otherwise provision 21 and any objections to any part of this agreement in its entirety are implicitly and explicitly hereby waived.

ADDITIONAL RULES AND REGULATIONS OF THE CITY OF _____ WHILE AT BASE

22. Participants must not enter the water before both a coach and the lifeguard are on duty. Participants may never swim unattended while at the pool.

23. Users may not engage in potentially destructive behavior. Horseplay, running, pushing others in, standing or sitting on kickboards will not be tolerated.

24. Participants must treat the facility and equipment with due care and respect. Do not sit on or play on diving boards, pool blankets or reels.

25. Participants must swim under lane lines and not over them. Do not sit on lane lines.

26. Diving is not allowed in water less than 5 feet.

27. While there are tarps in the pool, no one is allowed in the pool. Participants may help put swim tarps across the pool, but they may not swim under the tarps. NO EXCEPTIONS!

28. All participants must be escorted by the deck chaperone or a person designated by the deck chaperone; i.e., an adult parent, to the restrooms.

29. Leave the pool area clean with all equipment stored.

30. All base rules must be followed.

31. No parent or persons on behalf of any parent is allowed to contact anyone at the base to ask for a pass or permit on to the base. Do not ask the guards at the gate to let you on to the base for any reason whatsoever.

32. Children are not to change in the locker rooms and are not allowed in the locker rooms to use the restroom after 7:00 PM. Everyone should be off deck and the deck cleared no later than 8:20 PM as the lifeguards must close the facilities by 8:30 PM.

Minor Infractions consist of vulgar language, horseplay, not cooperating with the lifeguards and any verbal or physical abuse. City Lifeguards will give three warnings before suspension for minor violations within a six-month time period. This will include coaches, participants and spectators. Upon first suspension the individual will not be permitted to use the pool facility the next day. The second violation will result in a two-day suspension. Continued violations will result in three-day suspension. After the third suspension the City Staff will expel the individual from the base for the remainder of the season. If this is a parent, the child will be suspended from swimming with *__Name of Corporation__*, and will not be permitted to return.

Major Violations include destruction of property or facility, jeopardizing of safety, use of pool without prior approval, misconduct of organization members, and *non-observance of city policies* and this may result in a cancellation of use by *__Name of Corporation__* and others of the navy base. Therefore, any persons acting in any such manner and not fully complying with all the rules and regulations set forth by the city or the base whether set forth herein or not set forth herein, shall immediately be suspended as members of *__Name of Corporation__* , and shall not be allowed to swim with *__Name of Corporation__* thereafter. Parents engaging in such acts shall cause the immediate and irrevocable suspension of their child(ren) from *__Name of Corporation__* and their child(ren) shall thereafter not be allowed to swim with *__Name of Corporation.__* Dues paid in advance shall not be subject to refund.

Use of the Base may be cancelled at any time due to violation of any of the rules set forth by the City of _____ or the base, whether set forth now or in the future. Misuse of equipment, misconduct of organization members, and non-observance of City Policies are all cause for cancellation. Anyone causing such cancellation or causing a

call for a hearing on cancellation or for any other matter, shall immediately be suspended from membership of *Name of Corporation*

Questions shall be posted in writing and sent to *insert email address* and shall be forwarded to the entire board for comment.

I understand and agree to the above rules terms and conditions of *Name of Corporation* in exchange for the privilege of my child(ren), registered with this form, to participate in the activities and swimming program of *Name of Corporation*. I have explained to my child(ren) the terms of this agreement as they are pertinent to my child(dren) and (we) agree to abide by the rules and regulations as set forth above.

(Signature of Parent or Guardian)_____

Date:_____

Chapter Twenty-Three

Insurance and Medical Waivers

When it comes to insurance, if you are volunteering or on a board of directors, make it a point as to what your insurance requires in order to afford coverage for your swimmers and your coaches. One thing it most certainly will not cover, unless you pay extra for it. is insurance for the board of directors of the organization It will also not cover injuries sustained by your employees because you are required by law to purchase workers compensation to cover injuries that happen to your employees while they are engaged in the scope and practice of their work. You should also ascertain if your policy covers things such as sexual harassment of either children or adults.

The good guys' board I represented essentially found out they had no insurance for their organization at all, and no one at the local or national level seemed bothered by this because nothing bad had happened without it. There was no claim or occurrence, so no one was disturbed by this other than the good guys.

Insurance was void or voidable on several different levels. First, in order to have USA swimming insurance for the kids on the pool, every child swimming either had to have a USA swimming card, or they had to have been swimming with the team for less than thirty days and have signed a temporary waiver and release of claims and damages should a problem occur. If the child swimming under thirty days had a problem, he would not have been covered had an accident occurred, although others in the pool would still be covered. This is one reason why a temporary waiver was needed. The other reason a temporary or thirty day waiver was needed is because without it no one in the pool was covered. When the good guys took office, not all the children were members of USA Swimming simply because parents felt if their child wasn't competing, it wasn't necessary to join. Since the coach took no part in enforcing this rule prior to the good guys stepping on board, the team had been technically and actually uninsured whenever a child without a USA Swimming card was in the pool.

Of course none of that really mattered when it was found out one of the long term coaches for the swim team didn't have a coach's card, and he hadn't had a coach's card for years. In order to have USA Swimming insurance apply all coaches on deck must have a coach's card unless they are a student working on a temporary basis (for only thirty days or less) under the card of the head coach. Several years constitutes a period of time greater than thirty days, therefore the good guys board of directors inherited a swim team that had been without insurance for years. That was all right. Nothing bad happened. Because this coach went to swim meets, all insurance was also voided there which meant anything that happened would flow right back to the employing corporation, and if there was no valid corporate status, back to the board of the directors that had no protective corporate veil.

This means that you should get a copy of your insurance policy or policies and read the contents carefully. Determine the requirements of the policy or policies and make certain you comply with the terms of those policies. It really is not so hard to do. Mainly you will generally have to have a credentialed coach and make sure the coach supervises the children at all times and does not leave the children alone, even for a minute, even for a second.

For your coaches who are your employees, follow the law. Pay for workers compensation insurance.

For the board of directors of your organization?

Obtain board of directors insurance because they are working for you for free, this is something no one else wants to do, and they are doing everything they do for you and your children.

Remember that if you act irresponsibly or allow your coaches to act irresponsibly, your organization may be held responsible and if you do not have that corporate veil of protection, the liability may flow to your board of directors, which if you are reading this handbook, may be you.

Keep copies of sports membership cards with the children at all times if these cards are linked to your insurance. Keep original medical releases with the coach at all times in case first aid must be rendered or worse. Keep all the paperwork together and in one spot in a file with the coach so it is there when you need it, and make sure you have those emergency numbers and know exactly who to call.

A release puts a portion of the responsibility back onto the parent, but remember it is not something that absolves from all fault, and a parent generally cannot release the rights of the child who may come back at the age of eighteen (in the State of California) and bring a lawsuit on his own for injuries suffered. If you are not properly covered your only defense will be the contributory negligence of the parent in allowing the participation of the child, and this is an ugly picture to paint.

On the other hand, if you are an organization that has been warned there is a problem with your coach, (that he is a child molester, for example) and your board does nothing to resolve the problem, refusing to investigate or to take proper steps to prevent injury to a child, your organization will more than likely be found liable for damages when and if a child is molested, and because you were put on notice of the problem, actual and or constructively, and did nothing to prevent it, your insurance company may deny coverage even if sexual harassment is covered in your insurance policy.

A city or recreation department or anyone who gives access to pool time for this organization may also be liable if they have been given actual or constructive notice, as may the local and or national sports organization if they have been given actual or constructive notice and have refused to act responsibly.

"I don't believe it," is not justification or excuse. "It isn't up to me to take care of this," is also not justification or excuse. If you are informed of a problem or a situation that could an cause foreseeable harm to another and the outcome is reasonably foreseeable that if what you are told is true, or if you are able to investigate and discover the truth of it and do not do anything about it, even if you have governmental immunity, the fact that you have been put not notice of this foreseeable problem may make you liable for damages should an injury or other problem occur, because in not investigating the facts and in not acting to prevent the act you will have acted in a negligent manner.

To follow is what our waivers looked like.

MEDICAL INFORMATION AND WAIVER

-STRICTLY CONFIDENTIAL-

Mandatory for participation in *__Name of Organization's Team__*

The completion of this document is mandatory and the swimmer will not be allowed to swim unless it is kept current and on file. It is the responsibility parent or guardian of each swimmer to insure the accuracy of the information contained herein, except if that swimmer is over the age of 18 and/or is an emancipated minor child, and then it is the duty of the latter. It assumed each individual receiving this document speaks and understands English, and *__Name of Corporation__* is not responsible for any misunderstanding regarding the information requested herein, nor does it take any responsibility for any translation given an/or offered by any third party. If there is more than one swimmer in your family, please submit multiple copies to be filed.

SWIMMER:_____

ADDRESS_____

_____

PHONE NUMBER_____

PARENTS/GUARDIANS_____

ADDRESS(ES)_____

PHONE NUMBER(S)_____

ALTERNATIVE/EMERGENCY PERSON TO CALL IN EMERGENCY_____

PHONE NUMBER_____

MEDICAL COVERAGE_____

PHYSICIAN'S NAME_____

PHONE NUMBER OF PHYSICIAN_____

MEDICAL CONDITIONS OF WHICH EMERGENCEY PERSONELL AND COACHES SHOULD BE AWARE

_____

_____

PRIOR INJURIES THAT SWIMMING MAY EFFECT OR THAT MAY EFFECT SWIMMING:

_____

_____

ANY OTHER CONDITIONS, CIRCUMSTANCES (I.E., A,D.D., FAMILIAL SITUATION) THAT GUARDIANS WOULD LIKE TO CONFIDE TO COACHES THAT COULD EFFECT PRACTICES, FOCUS OR ATTITUDE OF THE SWIMMER:

_____

_____

_____

WAIVER mandatory signature required

I intending to be legally bound do forever hereby, for myself, my heirs, executors, administrators and assigns, waive, release and forever discharge any and all rights and claims for any damages of any kind whatsoever, medical or otherwise, which I or the minor for whom I sign hereunder, may hereafter accrue against ***Name of Organization*** and/or to its officers. representatives, agents, and successors and assigns with, or in entry in and arising out of participation in, travel to and returning from any swim practice, workout or event and relieve the same from any indemnification, liability or responsibility from any and all damage arising there from. I assume the risk involved in any and all activities, swim practices, workouts and events to which I or the minor child under the age of eighteen on whose behalf I sign this document may incur, knowing and fully realizing and recognizing all risks involved.

I further authorize emergency medical treatment as necessary, emergency medical transport, hospitalization and physicians care as necessary in my absence, and agree to be liable for payment of any services rendered and forever release, relieve and indemnify ***Name of Organization*** association for this and for any medical malpractice which may occur as a result of rendering any emergency or other medical aid.

Name of Swimmer: _____

Age of Swimmer_____

Date Signed_____

Signature of Parent/legal Guardian_____

Chapter Twenty-Four

The Honor Code

If you have kids that will be traveling to meets, tournaments, games or competitions, you should adopt some basic standards of behavior, because when the children are with the team under the supervision of a coach that you have hired or perhaps with the supervision of other team parents you may be doubly liable. First, you may be liable if something happens to the child (hence you will need a travel waiver); and second you may be held liable if the child commits some act of wrong while in your care. In other words if your chaperone or your coach negligently supervises the child, the organization may be held responsible. This is why some sort of an honor code should be put in place. The parameters of what is acceptable behavior must be clearly set forth, and very real consequences must apply for any honor code violation in order to give you honor code teeth and in order to show you are serious about having the children behave properly and do the right thing. In other words, you are mitigating damages, should they occur. If you have set no written boundaries, you have no proof as to what are your defining standards of proper behavior. Here is one honor code example.

(NAME OF TEAM) HONOR CODE....
MANDATORY…………….. SIGNATURES REQUIRED

The following Code of Honor must be adhered to by all swimmers. Failure to follow this code of honor may result in the following: 1) Team suspension for a period of time to be decided by the head coach and board of directors of (*Name of Organization)*; 2) Not being allowed to attend future competitions for a period of time to be decided by the head coach and the board of directors of (*Name of Organization*); or 3) Permanent expulsion from the team.. You will be subject to due process and you will have a noticed hearing and opportunity to be heard should you be charges with any violation of the team honor code or its rules prior to any disciplinary action being taken against you. At that time you may present you side of the facts along with any mitigating factors you may offer.

1. **(Name of team)** may travel as a team to competition as a team. Everyone is expected to behave. . The reputation of **(Name of Team)** is reflected by how you behave individually or within the group team, or with others.

2. The head coach holds the final word on any rules, regulations, or disciplinary actions.

3. You may not purchase or drink alcohol. You may not smoke or chew tobacco, or use any illegal drug or substance. You must excuse yourself from any individuals doing this, whether members of your team or not, and leave immediately and report the wrong to the head coach or your chaperone. If you do not do this you will be punished just as though you have engaged in the prohibited behavior.

4. You will not go to the room of a member of the opposite sex.

5. You must attend all team meetings and you must be prompt and punctual. You must be at the when you are told to be there for practice or warm-up or otherwise.

6. You may not leave your room once lights out time has occurred. You may not go anywhere without an adult who is in charge, or with your own parent(s).

7. Any damages or thievery incurred in a room will be at the expense of the swimmers in that room. You may not take anything from the room that you did not bring into it or you will be subject to discipline. You must conduct yourself with proper decorum and no loud or boisterous behavior will be allowed in your room. All phone calls must be made by credit card or made collect if made from the room, any additional phone access charges from the hotel will be paid by you.

..8 You will be polite in restaurants. Leave a 15% tip. If there has been a problem with the service, tell the coach or ask your adult supervisor what to do.

9. Follow all team rules regarding practice and meet behavior. Use no vulgar or offensive language. Use good manners!

This honor code is not all inclusive. If you have a question about how to behave, please direct your question to the adult in charge.

I agree to abide by the above Code of Conduct, and also agree that should I violate any of the rules of conduct as stated above, or act in any manner that is vulgar or offensive, that. I will take responsibility for my wrong and accept my sanction and punishment.

Swimmer_____ Dated_____

Parent _____ Dated_____

Chapter Twenty-Five

The Team Commitment Form

Every participant in a sport has his or her own level of commitment to the sport. Each level of commitment may be different. It is important to know the level of commitment of the swimmer and parent in order that the coach knows how to proceed with the child. The team commitment form may be used as a tool to begin a dialogue between parent and coach and to determine the direction the child is going in the sport. Most children think filling this form out is fun because it gives them a sense of importance, and because the parent is required to participate with the child in filling out the form, it gives the parent a chance to communicate with the child. The form should be used at least once a year and filled in by all newcomers to the team. Use of the form will enable the organization to see what it is the parent expects. In the long term this can avoid problems with parents who complain they did not get their money's worth, because the coach can sit down with the disappointed disgruntled parent or the board and discuss expectations and results in a rational manner. Parents always want the child to be a star. A child generally only wants to have fun. The team commitment can put the two perspectives together, and hopefully the child can have fun and progress while acting within his or her own personal expectations. It would be unusual for a parent to sue you corporation because of missed expectations, but it would not be impossible. You will still get the occasional stopped check from a parent who only wants to take advantage of the organization for a week or two of babysitting after school and that is another issue, but a happy and informed parent is less dangerous than a parent who is unhappy and disgruntled, and parents tend to be both of those things.

    My child started filling out this form when she was five. It helped her set surprising goals from a very early age, goals that surprised me because they were set so early. She was lucky to have coaches who loved and cared about her and who still love and care about her and interact with her to this day, even though she and they have regretfully moved on, and I enclose this trusty form as a tribute, of sorts, to them, because they were wonderful and they helped me learn all about my child and her sport. When my child began I swore she would not be pushed and I only wanted her to have fun and not to compete. My daughter, on the other hand, had a different idea, and is still competing in her sport ten years later! If we had not filled out this form together, I would have never known about her passion for her sport. I may not always be happy about her level of dedication being so strong, because it means there has to be a commitment of both time and expense from me, but she is a child who has never complained about going to practice, and a child that I had to promise to never punish by refusing to take her to practice. She works out in a gym now and runs and does many things all on her own initiative, just to develop herself so that she can perform her sport better. She is patient with herself and serious about her technique and asks for correction, and she has been asking for advice on her technique since she was six. Her early coaches explained everything to her in terms she could understand and would ask her, "Why do you think I am asking you to do that?" so that she always had to think about the how and why of what she was doing. She has had to be conscious of every part of her body and what it is doing, and she has been required to be responsible for herself and her things (although that part was not easy for her mother). My daughter is very tall, and her body has constantly changed and she does not always do as well as some of her piers, but she is patient about her development in the sport, hopes for the best and loves what she is doing.

Even if I have felt discouraged about her performance, she has never been discouraged because she has been taught to look at the long term development of herself and vies herself as being in competition with herself, more than with others. She does not understand why her peers cry when they don't do well, and looks for a lesson in what she does, even if it is not as good as she would have liked it to be. She experiments with her performance and is not afraid to take a chance and do something different, even if it means she goes slower, because she understands it will help in the long term. She also knows if a coach is a good coach or a bad coach, and I have learned to listen to her.

That said, I recommend this form for your organization and its children and parents. To me, it has been a window to my daughter's heart and soul. It was part of the beginning of who she was to become. She may never be the fastest or the best, but she will always love her sport because what she does, she does for herself and because she loves the sport, and for no one else, and for no other reason. Is this not what we all want for our children? My daughter's love of what she does, shows in her performance, and this is all that matters She stuffs her ribbons and medals into a drawer and doesn't think about them at all because the ribbons and the medals are in no way a measure of who she is or of where she is going.

My daughter's sport is swimming, but you can easily modify this form to suit your own sport.

I found this form in the happy days before I ran into the team with the trouble, the team that I desperately tried to protect and save. In the happy days we were with a team where we were like a family in a perfect place in space and time. If you are reading this book and you were a part of this time and space, you know who you are, and so I say, "Thank-you, .just for being you!"

But don't stop there. Parents need to make certain commitments too! This means if you want your parents to understand exactly what is expected of them you need to make things clear, and if the parents don't like the guidelines they are required to file, then they should be asked to leave because they do not belong on your team or in your organization. The kids need to know and understand they must follow rules of good sportsmanship, and the parents need to know and understand what your sport is attempting to do for the children. Remember it is all about the children and nothing less and nothing more.

Review the following document for an idea of what you might want to include in your team packets.

Name of Organization

TEAM COMMITMENT AGREEMENT FOR PARENTS AND SWIMMERS

It is mandatory that both parents and swimmers initial all points and that swimmers sign and date this document at its end. You do not have to agree to all items. This is to let the coaches know your level of commitment to (**Name of Team**).

1. A good practice begins with being on time, with my bathing suit on, ready to stretch at the time designated by the coaches.
   _____**I will do this.**

2. Proper equipment is essential to a proper workout. Swimsuit, cap, goggles, fins, hand paddles and water bottle are standard equipment.

   _____**I will have all my equipment marked with my name and carry it with me to every practice.**

3. The rules for warm ups are bi-lateral breathing, flip turns, perfect streamlining and strong kicks, two strokes off the wall before breathing, no stopping and no fooling around.
   _____**I agree to swim warm ups this way**.

4. Swim equipment is my responsibility, not the responsibility of my parents, brother or sister.
   _____**I will have my equipment at every practice**.

5. Our time in the water is relatively limited, but the pursuit of excellence is our goal

During practices,

_____I will pay attention, listen, and swim workouts as described by my coach, and I will not fool around and hold up practice.

6. Endurance is built by consistent swimming. Swimming skills are learned and perfected progressively; therefore, all practices are important.
_____I will attend every practice to which I am committed.
_____I will let coaches know in advance that I am going to miss a practice.
_____I will let coaches know in writing I will be on vacation, or if I will miss a meet.

7. The best way for a swimmer to observe his/her improvements, and for coaches to gauge improvements or gaps in training is to attend swim meets.
_____I will swim at least one swim meet per month.

8. Cooperation is necessary for getting swim meet entries in on time.
_____I will get my entry money and my entry cards in by the due date.

9. Information is sent by email or posted on (insert web address) or given to me by the coach pertinent to training, meet notices, parties and other special events.
_____I will check my email and the *Name of Organization* website regularly.
_____I will put information or papers given to me by the coach in my swim bag and deliver them to my parents the same day.

10. When Rough Water Swim Practice begins, it is a well known fact that many swimmers are fearful of the new challenge. It is a very beneficial asset to the team and well worth the effort.
_____When rough water practices start I will try the new experience.

Printed Name_____Signature_____Date:_____
   participant

I will support my child in all of the above and not interfere with the coaching process. I will help my child become responsible for himself or herself, and I will give my child words of encouragement and love.

Printed
Name_____Signature_____Date:_____
        Parent

Good Sportsmanship is the ability to win without arrogance
and to lose without complaint.

Sportsmanship Rules
Kids: Initial if you agree

_____ If I make a mistake I won't pout or make excuses. I will learn from it and be ready for the rest of the competition.

_____ If a teammate makes a mistake, I will offer encouragement, not criticism.

_____ I will respect the efforts of everyone involved who made the competition possible, including my parents, the coaches, the officials, and the directors of the competition.

_____ I will be polite at all times, and say please and thank you, always using the best of manners.

_____ I will encourage my teammates, accept the calls of the officials and conduct myself with a positive attitude,

_____ I will make no excuses for mistakes and bad behavior. I will accept responsibility for all of my actions, both good and bad.

_____ I will not gloat or act arrogant if I win, and if I lose I will accept the loss with grace and dignity and without complaint.

_____ I promise to compete fairly and to abide by all the rules of the sport.

Parents: Initial if you agree

_____ I will encourage my child and praise them just for being a participant.

_____I will teach my child what it means to be a part of a team and to take responsibility for being a part of a team.

_____I will always look for the good in what my child has done, and I will not criticize my child for not winning.

_____I will tell my child that I love him just because…and help him learn from his mistakes by allowing the coach to point out ways he can improve and by staying out of the work of the coach.

_____I will remember this is about my child and not about me, and I will emphasize this sport is for fun and the concept of fun over winning.

_____I will be an example for my child and not gloat when he wins, or complain when he loses, and I will treat the coaches, the officials and everyone involved in the competition and the sport with respect and courtesy, without criticism or complaint when things do not go as I think they should have gone, remembering that I stand in the shoes of a parent and my role is the unique role of support and encouragement.

The above was adapted by permission from documents provided by La Mesa Swim Association's former aquatic's supervisor, Jill Lapp along with head coach Elizabeth Fletcher, creators of the above concept. For additional information see www.charactercounts.org/sports and *Athletes for a Better World* at www.aforbw.org. It is also suggested that you read *It's Just a Game!* (*Youth Sports and Self Esteem: A Guide for Parents*), by Dr. Darrell Burnett, Authors' Choice Press, www.iUniverse.com, and purchase Dr. Burnett's 20 item Parent Checklist which includes Dr. Burnett's audio cassette, *Hey, Mom and Dad, It's Just a Game!* published by Fun Again Press, from which La Mesa Swim Association adapted its parent commitment checklists and from which, in part, it gained its inspiration. See: www.djburnett.com

Everything You Never Wanted To Know About Your Nonprofit Corporation

Chapter Twenty-Six
It Can't All Be Bad

There are teams out there that must be problem free. As I explained earlier, I had my own daughter on such a team for several years, and I would like to believe this was not just a fluke, but I must tell you that when the head of the aquatics program left, the team disappeared shortly after. The problem was that the level of commitment it takes to run a really effective program is quite high and very time consuming, even if you are getting paid to do it. The team that was perfect in time and place happened to be a recreation team that was a part of the local and national scheme and also participated in swim meets and other events at the municipal and state level, The director was extremely involved and knew the strengths and weaknesses of each child, had coaches meetings with the various level coaches once a week, had notebooks with the kids times all charted, notebooks with all the swim cards neatly in place accompanied by all the medical releases and phone numbered on the deck at all times. These coaches were so well informed that they knew how to explain to the individual child how they should swim according to their past performances and could sit down and show the child on paper why and how a particular thing should and could be done.

This is why what I ended up in was so utterly shocking. Nothing was in order. There were no medical waivers on deck. There were no swimmers cards on deck. Notebooks were kept of swims, but these were not used in relation to the workouts, much less in relation to any pattern of how to swim an event, or how to meet any goal set by the child.

I went from a well structured swim organization to an organization that was falling apart and I didn't know it. The problem is the child becomes involved and attached to his teammates, the coaches, and team parents, and parents develop relationships of a social nature among themselves. If you child is committed to the sport, this may even be a five or six days a week commitment, and so everything begins to revolve around the sport, eating, homework, bedtime and even bath or shower time (which may also be at the sport's site and part of the socialization ritual, as it is for swimmers).

It is because the sports thing is so socialized that recognizing a problem becomes so difficult. Sometimes it is a good idea to express your suspicions to someone you trust (as in the case of suspected child molestation), to see what they think. However, I must admit that when parents bounced suspicions off me, I ignored them, so it is probably just better to trust your own instincts.

Or you can do as Swimming Australia Lt. does and incorporate the following document or a similar one into your team package and coach hiring contracts. In fact, I would take the matter once step further requiring the declaration to also specify "no such acts as outlined above have been engaged in by the undersigned, attempted or solicited."

SAL MEMBER PROTECTION POLICY
PROHIBITED PERSON DECLARATION

The Swimming Australia Member Protection Policy makes it a breach of the policy for a Prohibited Person (defined as a person who has been convicted of a serious sex offence) to work or seek work in the following roles:

- **Coaches who are appointed or seeking appointment (whether employed, contracted or otherwise) for reward;**
- **Volunteer personnel appointed or seeking appointment, who will or are likely to travel with teams of competitors under 18 years of age; and**
- **Persons appointed or seeking appointment to a role in which that person is likely to have individual and unsupervised contact with competitors under 18 years of age (for example, a team manager).**

The swimming Australia Member Protection Policy also makes it a breach of the policy to appoint, or continue to appoint, a person to a role set out above:

- **Without first obtaining this declaration; or**
- **Where this declaration reveals the person is a prohibited person.**

The Swimming Australia Member Protection Policy defines a Serious Sex Offence to mean an offence involving sexual activity or acts of indecency or acts of indecency including but not limited to:

- **Rape**
- **Indecent assault**

- Sexual assault
- Assault with intent to have sexual intercourse
- Incest
- Sexual penetration of a child under the age of 16
- Indecent act with a child under the age of 16
- Sexual relationship with a child under the age of 16
- Sexual offences with people of impaired mental functioning
- Abduction and detention
- Procuring sexual penetration by threats or fraud
- Procuring sexual penetration of child under 16
- Bestiality
- Soliciting acts of sexual penetration or indecent acts
- Promoting or engaging in acts of child prostitution
- Obtaining benefits from child prostitution
- Possession of child pornography
- Publishing child pornography and indecent articles

Declaration

I am aware that I am ineligible to work or seek work in the roles set out above if I have been convicted of a Serious Sex Offence, as defined in the Swimming Australia Member Protection Policy.

I have read and understand the above information in relation to the Swimming Australia Member Protection Policy and understand my responsibilities and obligations under it.

I declare that I am not a person prohibited under the Swimming

Australia Member Protection Policy from working or seeking work in the roles set out above.

I acknowledge that I am required to advise the CEO or the most senior manager of the organization appointing me immediately upon becoming a prohibited person.

_____
Print Name

_____
Signature
Date:
Note: Seek legal advise if you are unsure of your status

Parent/Guardian Consent (in respect of person under the age of 18 years)

I have read and understood the declaration provided by my child. I confirm and warrant that the contents of the declaration provided by my child are true and correct in every particular.

_____
Name   Signature
Date

The above has been reprinted with the express permission of Swimming Australia Lt

Chapter Twenty-Seven
So What Else Do You Have To Do?

The main thing you have to do once the corporation is all correctly formed and you are following all the rules is to make sure all your governmental paperwork is complete and up to date. This means, of course that you need to make your quarterly payments on any money withheld from employee paychecks and make certain you keep that money segregated from your working capital. Remember it is not your money to use, borrow, steal or keep; and if you find someone on your board is suing, borrowing or stealing that money, call the proper authorities and then let the authorities straighten out the matter. Remember if you are not a part of the solution, you become a part of the problem. Do not be stupid. Do not involve yourself in the continuing commission of a felony, even if it is all too difficult to believe. Anyone who has nothing to hide will readily open the books and explain, and if someone is not forthcoming they have a reason, and the reason is not on the side of good.

The first thing to remember is that if the tax exempt organization brings in or is expected to bring in at least $25,000 a year, then the organization will be required to file an annual information return. This means most organizations involved in child sports that pay coaches will not be exempt from filing because the organization is more than likely paying its coaches at least that amount or more, and it is the gross receipts that are counted, not the net profit. In other words if the organization pays its coach $30,000 a year, it obviously had to bring in over $25,000 to pay the $30,000.00 to the coach. The IRS has a publication that explains all the record keeping required for a tax exempt organization, Publication 4221.

The form your team's tax exempt organization must file annually is Form 990. If your organization is very small you may be able to file form 990-EZ, the short version of Form 990. This was, in fact the form that started our organization downfall as the treasurer (who had not filed the form for years) became worried when I, as pro bono counsel for the board of directors asked to see the 990 Forms, sending her into a state of panic and team take-over.

When are you required to file the form?

If your nonprofit organization meets the requirements requiring filing it will be required to file the Form 990 or Form 990-EZ by the 15th day of the 5th month after the end of the accounting period. The form instructions explain where to send the form.

What will happen if the organization fails to file a Form 990?

A tax-exempt organization that fails to file a required return is subject to a penalty of $20 a day for each day the failure continues. The same penalty applies if the organization fails to give correct and complete information or required information on the organization's return and the maximum penalty on any single return is $10,000 or 5 percent of the organization's gross receipts for the yea, whichever is less. . If the organization has gross receipts in excess of $1,000,000, the penalties are increased to $100 per day with a maximum penalty of $50,000; however, it would be unlikely that a child's sports team would have gross receipts in excess of one million dollars.

Every organization with employees must also file and the proper forms in relation to their employees. and make quarterly payments to the IRS for FUTA (federal unemployment tax) and FICA (social security); Each state also has it's own particular filing requirements, and if you fail to comply with the requirements you may lose you tax exempt status. The IRS requires the filing of Form 940, Employers Federal Unemployment (FUTA) tax return, and Form 941 Employers Quarterly Federal Tax return, whether or not you are tax exempt. It is the organization that is tax exempt, and not the employees of the organization. Every employer is required to comply with reporting and withholding requirements of the state in which the organization is incorporated as well as with the federal filing requirements.

Our problem was our treasurer had not only not made the quarterly payments as required, she had not filed the Form 990 for years! At a penalty of up to $10,000 per Form 990 not filed, (not being in the million dollar income category, it is simple to see why the board of directors became gravely concerned. Of course as the IRS officer explained to me it might be possible to get penalties and interest waived if we said our treasurer was nuts.

There were also the state penalties, however, and the mere amounts missing and/or not forwarded as required after being allegedly withheld from the employee paychecks were of such magnitude as to virtually render the organization insolvent. However, no one wanted to accept this obvious fact at the local level, and because the
local level refused to address these issues, the national level would not address them stating it was outside the jurisdiction of the national level.

Now we have lost our team and organization and it is being run by others who are not paying the governmental entities as of the time of this writing, who blame those who discovered the problem for the problem and who have rationalized there is no problem at all because they don't owe taxes. They are correct, of course. They are, after all, tax exempt. However, this does not justify or excuse the failure to properly forward money withheld from employee paychecks and held in sacred trust, money that does not belong to the organization and never did belong to the
organization and money that if it ever truly existed has a great deal of it missing!

Do not let this happen to you! For additional information please go to http://www.irs.gov/charities/charitable/article/0,,id=122670,00.html and simply follow the underlined sections to their links. I could write more here, but it would be a waste of time and paper. The main thing to remember is that you need to follow all the rules and that you need to follow all the rules, or you could get yourself not only out in the cold without your organization, but you could also get yourself behind bars in prison, personally liable for what you did not stand up to prevent. Do not for one minute think it could never happen to you because everybody does it. If all the cars are speeding down the freeway, if you are the only one stopped and given a ticket, you will not be able to excuse yourself by saying everyone else was doing it. Sadly, unless you have a strong case for selective prosecution, which is very difficult to argue, you will go down if the cop decides to pull you over, and in the case of the IRS it is a problem waiting to happen.

Chapter Twenty-Eight
The Devil Made Me Do It!

You always need to do the right thing, even if everyone turns against you. When you do the right thing, no matter how politically unpopular, you will be doing everything possible to protect yourself from both civil and criminal liability. In fact those that were told over and over again of our problem by me, and chose to ignore what I told them cannot feign ignorance. Ignorance of the law also does not justify or excuse the commission of a crime, or the continuing commission of a crime. If money belongs to the state or to the IRS because it was withheld from paychecks upon which your employees have filed tax returns and either applied on paper those funds to a tax debt or accepted refund, it is the property of the government and is not a part of the assets of the organization. When money is not forwarded as required, it is in essence stolen. Those that keep the money and use it for any purpose other than that for which it was intended become thieves, and those that assist in the procurement of funds so owing become aiders and abettors in the commission of a crime, or in our case in the continuing commission of a crime, should the state and/or federal governments decide to prosecute. It will not matter if advice of legal counsel was the basis for this, and it will not matter what civil or administrative decisions have come down from the boards of the various governing sports organizations. In fact, those sports organizations may be held negligently or criminally liable in facilitating the commission of crimes as sports organizations and their governing bodies do not have governmental immunity as does a city, a public hospital, police, firefighters, and the like. In fact, chances are if legal counsel gave any advice other than to forward the money withheld, they have advised the continuing commission of a crime, and would be liable to all those they so advised because they have committed malpractice of such a serious nature as to threaten the status of their licenses to practice law. They may also be charged with participation in the criminal act.

It does not matter if everyone does it. It only matters that it is wrong. If there is nothing to hide, open the books and prove there is nothing to hide. When the IRS says it has not been paid anything for years and that years when money was paid quarterly it came in without paperwork, and attorneys say there is no problem the day after you have heard the contrary from the mouth of the IRS horse, and no one will believe you when you tell them the truth, then they bring the peril upon themselves. You cannot help them, even if you are an attorney. You are not God. They all become thieves because they refuse to do right and correct a wrong. Christ was crucified for being different and for espousing right. Can you expect any less from your peers?

"Be strong and of good courage, for the Lord, thy God is with you."

Let's face it, we are talking about a kid's team, not Fort Knox, and anyone who would steal from a kid's team is stealing from children. It is not much ado about nothing. It is much ado about doing right.

My advice is no matter how much you are tempted, do not get involved. Do not volunteer. You will not pass go. You will not win $200. You will lose the game and your heart may be broken. However, the truth is I didn't listen to my own advice, so I don't expect you as the reader to listen to my advice either. Therefore, if this handbook helps just one person or prevents just one organization from going inexplicably awry as ours did, then it is all worth it.

You must put the blade into the fire to make the blade strong.

Chapter Twenty-Nine

Exactly What Does the Law and the IRS Say?

IRS Commissioner, Mark Everson says, "Failure to pay unemployment taxes is stealing from the employees of the business. The IRS pursues business owners who don't follow the law and those who embrace these schemes face civil or criminal sanctions." See http://www.irs.gov/newsroom/article/0,,id=122521,00.html

The IRS realizes that maybe businesses just intend to borrow from the trust fund of money withheld from paychecks to keep the business going and then just don't pay it back. Suddenly the amount is so great everything has snowballed out of control and the business faces bankruptcy. The IRS realizes this can happen, but it does not excuse the act. In our case our board clearly faced insolvency. The board believed it would need to liquidate the underlying organization, but could and would keep the team. We were admonished by the local sport's governing organization overseeing all the local swim teams, based on the argument of the opposition that the organization could not possibly be insolvent with $20,000 in the bank. It sounded good, but the money did not belong to the organization and no one would listen.

In our situation some things were different. No one ever knew where the money went or if it was ever there at all. We had a treasurer who reported each month all was OK, that money was being sent in for quarterly payments and that all bills were being paid, a report under which the Board of Directors were allowed to justifiably and reasonably rely under the laws of our state, so long as they had no notice otherwise or reasons of suspicion. The problems came when the head coach was moving from the state and reported to the board of directors the IRS had no record of his employment for over four years. Once this individual reported this problem to the board, then they could no longer justifiably rely on the representations of the treasurer and her monthly reports. They were on notice something may be wrong and a duty of care was triggered that necessitated investigation of the matter, less they become personally and individually liable for the acts of the treasurer, whether innocent and by mistake, inadvertence or neglect or by a part of a scheme and/or device to defraud

It does not matter now what the reasons were or why the treasurer did what she did. If she took money to fund the day to day business of the organization, no matter how well intentioned her scheme, it was still a theft because the money did not belong to the organization. When $20,000 was sitting in a bank and over $50,000 was allegedly withheld from paychecks and not forwarded to the IRS and to the state, that

$20,000 should have been immediately turned over to the proper authorities. It should not have been claimed as an asset of the organization. It thereafter became the duty of the board of directors of the organization to see to it that they did everything possible to get the funds to the proper owner of those funds, lest they become personally and individually liable for the loss of the funds. Once the takeover group prevented access to the bank account and then to the PO box where the funds were sent, and once they thereafter took possession of those funds and (knowing all of the above because they were put on actual notice of the above) did not forward them to the IRS or to the state, and claimed them as the property of the takeover organization, they all became thieves involved in a scheme or artifice to defraud the employees of the organization, the state and the IRS, because they stole the money from the employees of the organization and to the extent those funds were returned to the employees in tax refunds or credited to owed taxes, they stole from the IRS and the state.

This is not something that takes a genius IQ to figure out. All it takes is honesty, a willingness to see and accept the facts as they are and a bit of common sense. The response of the local overseeing sports organization was to get rid of me, the whistle blower, with utmost urgency, for as long as possible, and to completely ignore the underlying acts of a long time friend they were trying to protect; however, in the end, they will actually cause her more harm than good. It is always better to accept responsibility for wrong and to make correction, and even the courts of law will recognize that!

Do not let your nonprofit organization fall into this perilous trap. The law says it is wrong. Do not be tempted to borrow either for yourself or for the organization money that does not belong to either you or the organization. Do not kid yourself. No matter how good your intentions, if you do this you are a thief. Come clean. Make it right! Remember, "Thou shalt not steal!" Don't use this money for attorneys' fees, and remember that attorneys who knowingly take these funds are eating poisonous fruit. When you are up to your neck in alligators, it is difficult to get out of the swamp.

Chapter Thirty

Keeping the Alligators Out of the Swamp

If you want to keep the alligators out of the swamp then you must play by the rules and the rules are clear. The IRS rules give both employer and employee the responsibility for collecting and submitting withholding taxes. While it is true the employer is supposed to hold the money withheld from employee paychecks in trust to be submitted to the IRS, if the employer does not do this, it becomes the responsibility of the employee to collect and pay his or her own withholding taxes. While you may believe those statements sent to you from the IRS regarding your social security are just so much junk mail to be thrown out, the statements actually serve a greater purpose. The greater purpose of those statements is that if you do not see a record of employment with your employer, or if the amounts indicated as submitted do not coincide with your records, you must notify the IRS and/or your employer to take steps to rectify the matter, or in the end you could technically be held liable for missing money that was actually stolen from you by your employer. I am not saying this will happen, but it could happen, because the letters the IRS send to you are putting you on notice of what the IRS has in its records and if there is nothing in that social security benefit statement you receive, then your employer has not followed the law and since it is the responsibility of both the employee and the employer to pay the withholding amounts, than you can see where the problem may arise. . Of course you are allowed to rely on the representations set forth in your W2's, but if your W2's do not coincide with the social security projected benefits statement you receive or if there is no record of your employment, then in the very least you could be losing what you thought you had in future benefits. I have been told by the IRS they will go after the employer for the employee, but the IRS is the IRS, so anything is actually possible.

The IRS defines the responsibility of the employee and Employees who do not have taxes withheld and do not send in these amounts on their own , are liable for the taxes and may not qualify for Social Security, Medicare, or unemployment benefits. The IRS expects the employee to oversee and police what the employer is doing as to the withholding and to take certain steps to assure the taxes that are supposed to be withheld from paychecks are withheld and sent to the IRS. If the employee has a problem he should call the IRS at 1-800-829-1040 and report the problem. The employee also needs to contact the employer and make sure the wages are properly withheld because if the IRS is unable to collect the withholding from the employer, then as stated above, the employee is still responsible for paying both the income tax and the FICA tax. In other words, the employer, by not forwarding the taxes is stealing from the employee.

If the employee does not get a W-2, (in our situation W-2s were issued, but nothing was withheld), then the employee needs to complete form 4852 and fill in as best possible from paychecks and the like, amounts made and amounts withheld and attach the form to his tax return in substitution of the W-2 form.

The bottom line is if the employer does not pay the taxes and/or refused to pay the unemployment taxes an/or withhold the money as required IRS is not able to collect the taxes from the employer, then the employee still has the responsibility to pay income tax and is also responsible for the FICA tax. .

The IRS considers this to be a serious matter and will and can impose a serious price, subjecting employers to both civil and criminal penalties. The employees may not be able to collect social security when the time comes, or may have benefits substantially reduced and they may end up without Medicare benefits when those benefits are needed the most. The result is that in the end the compliant employers who follow the law end up footing the bill for the non complaint, and all our taxes end up being raised to take up the slack. You may not like paying taxes; however, you must render unto Caesar that which is Caesar's!

This is why the board of directors I represented wanted to do the right thing and to take all steps necessary to follow the law and not become complicit in continuing criminal acts, and why I as counsel did not advise the continuing commission of this crime. The only way to stop the crime was to send the money to the proper governmental authorities and not to keep is. This was our stance from the beginning and we said over and over again this is what we wanted to do; however, the local governing board of our sport simply decided we wanted to liquidate the corporation to fund our new corporation, when this was not supported at all by the facts in that we had agreed with the state agency to put the disputed funds in trust for the benefit of creditors, governmental and otherwise and the state agency had agreed to give all concerned proper notice. The fact of this agreement was scoffed at, ridiculed and twisted so that nothing made any sense and everyone who did not support the agreement, or acted in such a manner as to prevent this agreement from moving forward, became complicit in assisting with a criminal as well as civil fraud. If you are reading this and you were one of these people, and if you are getting nervous, you should be nervous, very, very nervous!

What they all needed to do was to: "Get those alligators out of that swamp!" .

Chapter Thirty-One
The Law is the Law, And Sorry Folks, But What I Am Saying Is True!

The Internal Revenue Code Section 3203, Deduction of Tax from Compensation, states in pertinent part that the taxes imposed by Section 3203;

". . . shall be collected by the employer of the taxpayer by deducting the amount of the taxes from the compensation of the employee as and when paid. An employer who is furnished by an employee a written statement of tips (received in a calendar month) pursuant to section 6053(a) to which paragraph (3) of section 3231(e) is applicable may deduct an amount equivalent to such taxes with respect to such tips from any compensation of the employee (exclusive of tips) under his control, even though at the time such statement is furnished the total amount of the tips included in statements furnished to the employer as having been received by the employee in such calendar month in the course of his employment by such employer is less than $20."

Section 3102 Deduction of Tax from Wages further specifies:

"The tax imposed by section 3101 shall be collected by the employer of the taxpayer, by deducting the amount of the tax from the wages as and when paid."

There are many instances of enforcement and investigation of the failure to comply with the above in the public records.

For example, on August 20, 2004 in Miami, Florida Laurie Gregorio was sentenced, in part to fifteen months in prison and ordered to pay $421,541 in restitution after pleading guilty to conspiring against the IRS through tax evasion because she failed to forward more than $200,000 in taxes withheld from employee paychecks; and on May 21, 2004, in Omaha, Nebraska, Michael Dane Webb was sentenced to serve five months in prison, followed by five months of home detention. Webb had previously pled guilty to a felony for willfully failing to account for and pay over employment taxes. He admitted in his plea agreement he withheld money from employees' wages for Social Security, Medicare, and income taxes, and did not report, deposit or pay over those withholdings taxes to the IRS during 1996, 1997 and 1998. This allowed him to accumulate about $120,000, but it also put him in jail with a felony conviction.

In our case somehow everyone thought this was OK because we were a nonprofit group, but a felonious act is a felonious act, no matter where it happens; and stealing is stealing and thieves are without excuse. A rose is still a rose, no matter what you want to call it! Please see: http://www.irs.gov/compliance/enforcement/article/0,,id=106707,00.html for further examples.

Each state will also have their own laws regarding withholding from paychecks and below is the applicable California law. For the specific laws of you state, please consult your own legal counsel for advice..

The State of California Unemployment Insurance Code Section 986 states in pertinent part that each employer shall

". . . . withhold in trust the amount of his workers' contributions from their wages at the time the wages are paid, shall show the deduction on his payroll records, and shall furnish each worker with a statement in writing showing the amount which has been deducted, in such form and at such times as may be prescribed.

(2) Hold in trust the amount of his workers' contributions, at the time their wages are paid... .

(b) Each employer shall transmit all such contributions withheld or held in trust to the department for the Disability Fund, in addition to his own contributions for the Unemployment Fund, pursuant to authorized regulations."

California further provides for penalty under California Unemployment Code Section 117.5 and states in pertinent part

"Any person who, within the time required by this **code**, willfully fails to file any return or report, or to supply any information with intent to evade any tax imposed by this **code**, or who, willfully and with like intent, makes, renders, signs, or verifies any false or fraudulent return, report, or statement or supplies any false or fraudulent information, is punishable by imprisonment in the county jail not to exceed one year, or in the state prison, or by a fine of not more than twenty thousand dollars ($20,000), or by both the fine and imprisonment, at the discretion of the court".

California further defines who may be charged under the code in California Unemployment Code Section 2129 and states in that section:

" For the purposes of this chapter, "person" includes, a claimant for benefits and any officer, employee, director, partner, or agent having charge of the affairs of any employer or employing unit with regard to the violation which occurred. "Person" also includes both natural persons and legal entities. *More than one person may be charged with violations under this chapter, where control of the affairs of the employing unit, or employer, is shared by more than one person."* (emphasis added)

This is why you must be careful when you volunteer to take a position on a nonprofit organization board of directors because more than one person can be charged with committing this wrong where control of the affairs of the employing unit,(in our case our board of directors was the employing unit) is shared by more than one person. Because the board was charged under the bylaws with the running of the day to day business of the corporation and because they were charged with notice of the treasurer not performing her duties properly and as she had represented to the board, the ones was on them to do the right thing and to make certain the proper governmental authorities received the money held in trust, even if it meant bringing a civil action against the offending treasurer if she would not cooperate in making restitution to the state and to the IRS of money that either belonged to those governmental authorities or to the employees of the nonprofit corporation because it was money withheld from paychecks in trust and not a part of the assets of the corporation.

It's a dangerous proposition, volunteering; and it certainly is no walk in the park when in order to do the right thing you are attacked, defamed, falsely accused of wrongful actions and have your livelihood threatened as was mine, while you expend endless hours of work throughout a year of sleepless nights. Had I wanted all of this I could have continued with my full time practice of law and not gone into semi-retirement to rear my last child. At least then I would have been making some money for all my aggravation.

Unfortunately I have a problem. I cannot run away from a wrong. Besides, my husband had taken on the presidency of the board of directors and when this was discovered this board had only been in power four months. There was no choice. We had already accepted the slippery slope and were now taking the ride of our lives down that slope.

Ironically, in all of these administrative bodies declaring the takeover of the team valid, they took away the power of the board of directors I represented to do anything and turned over both the assets and the liabilities to the takeover group. While everyone was prepared to take on the extreme responsibility and challenge of making all of this right through the taking of appropriate legal steps, all of that was removed from our power. By removing all of that fro our power we became free of the responsibility because the responsibility was taken from our hands. The board may still be named in an action by the IRS and the EDD as may all the boards preceding during the time of the wrongful actions of the treasurer, but at least there is a strong and valid defense that this board spent a year doing everything they could to obtain the money from the bank account and to get that money to the IRS and EDD!

Even the ability to take civil action was removed as to the collection of these funds not forwarded and not in the account, because the local governing sport's body along with the national governing body of the sport went along and essentially supported the bad guys by finding in their favor that the organization was theirs, taking standing to bring a civil action and/or a criminal complaint away from the good guys. Even the post office fit into their mix and each bad decision relied on the bad decision that came before it with the ultimate result of defrauding the State of California and the IRS, with each entity passing the buck to the other and refusing to look at the totality of the circumstances. It was all so simple. Money was taken from paychecks of employees, income tax withholding, FICA and the like and it was not sent to the IRS or the state of California as required under law. Whatever was done with the money, the short story is that it was stolen from the paychecks of employees. This is wrong. .One of the employees to whom this was done over several years was one of the coaches who were terminated by this board, further complicating his position in all of this because he then will have no excuse when the IRS or state tells him he must now pay all that withholding himself because he assisted in the continuing commission of criminal acts and fraud and under law the employee is charged with making sure the proper governmental entities are sent the money withheld from his own paycheck.

If you want to be in America, then you have to follow its laws and rules, at least you are supposed to follow the rules. You may get away with something for awhile, but you can't get sway with doing wrong forever.

To those who stole our team and engaged in all these things, what kind of an example is this for your children, to do wrong and fly in the face of what is right and just?

Check out California Penal Code Section 484 and read, a bit further. Were you aware any taking of property over $400 was grand theft when you conspired in all of this? Why yes you were, because I told you so and I gave you all the code sections. If you didn't read them personally, then you are still charged with knowledge because I gave all of this to your attorneys when I made all those offers of settlement trying to get the IRS and the State of California money that belonged to them, money taken from employees paychecks in trust, money estimated in excess of $50,000.. Maybe you should ask your attorneys all about it. Oh yes, I forgot, they don't believe me. Besides, they wanted to be paid, and they didn't charge much. They only asked you for your immortal souls. But this is just my unprofessional opinion, this soul thing. Souls are up to God. He's the only professional in the area of souls. I worked for free, and I paid dearly for it, but it was only a worldly thing. I still have my soul!

So read Penal Code Section 484 again, and this time, please pay attention:

"484. (a) Every person who shall feloniously steal, take, carry, lead, or drive away the personal property of another, or who shall fraudulently appropriate property which has been entrusted to him or her, or who shall knowingly and designedly, by any false or fraudulent representation or pretense, defraud any other person of money, labor or real or personal property, or who causes or procures others to report falsely of his or her

wealth or mercantile character and by thus imposing upon any person, obtains credit and thereby fraudulently gets or obtains possession of money, or property or obtains the labor or service of another, is guilty of theft"

What is grand theft?

"487. Grand theft is theft committed in any of the following cases: (a) When the money, labor, or real or personal property taken is of a value exceeding four hundred dollars ($400) . . ."

What is the punishment for grand theft in the State of California?

"489. Grand theft is punishable as follows: (a) When the grand theft involves the theft of a firearm, by imprisonment in the state prison for 16 months, 2, or 3 years. (b) In all other cases, by imprisonment in a county jail not exceeding one year or in the state prison."

A house on a hill cannot long be hid. If the bad guys get away with what they have done, then my faith in the legal system will be shaken again, but I will remain forever the naive optimist, trusting others a bit less, having my confidence in fellow man shaken and thinking God must be looking down with tears in his eyes at the general state of affairs in this beautiful world he created as he sees man destroy both himself and the world through a series of senseless, stupid and inexplicable wrongs.

Sign me as the only lawyer I know now that has the unfortunate disadvantage of not being able to lie in a world of liars, gypsies, tramps and thieves, (although I like gypsies). .

I have been practicing law for over twenty years now, and everything just seems to get worse, and worse out there in the world, but that said, the above and the contents of this book are the opinions of one attorney only and are not meant to give specific advice on any single area of the law. For specific advice on any area of the law, please contact your own legal counsel as laws vary from state to state.

This is my story, it's sad but it's true; and truth is an absolute defense to any charges of defamation, so if you are someone who recognizes yourself in this book, go away and suck on an egg. All names have been omitted for the sheer protection of the just, the right, and the good, no matter what their political affiliations and positions may be. Even my own name as author is a nom de plume. To those attorneys who have laughed at me, belittled me, yelled, chastised me, boiled me in oil, made my life miserable, and made fun of me for telling the truth, and for doing right, I bet you never thought you would see yourselves, at least the essence of who and what you are, memorialized in print. To you and to those bad guys you represent, I say thank you for setting me upon a new course. God does have perfect planning, and I am praying for your immortal souls.

No wonder no one likes attorneys. I am one and I can't stand them either!

This is not the end, it is only the beginning. Right must and will prevail over wrong; and to those of you too scared to do anything and too scared to stand behind your convictions, I say stop acting like a turtle and come out of your shells or the alligators in the swamp will get you and will eat you up! And as to the former president of our organization who sat on the local sports committee in judgment of me, our board of directors and the team, because this first began way back on your watch, (the not forwarding of funds withheld in trust to proper governmental authorities), and because the IRS had even called you directly just a few months before all this was discovered, giving you constructive notice something was wrong, to you I say good luck to you with the IRS and the State of California. I hope you have a good attorney, because you should have listened, and you should not have been a hypocrite. You should have done the right thing, not the wrong thing, but perhaps your sense of moral superiority just got in the way.

To all you superior, opinionated moralists I say review your sense of morality and apply the law.

For myself I say, "Free at last, free at last, thank God almighty, I am free at last!"

Thanks Art, for all your help. You know who you are! (And by the way, in case you are wondering, Art is one of the good guys!)

By the way, I like writing better than practicing law, because I can say exactly what I want to say as long as it's the truth; and guess what else? You bad guys can't stop me! It's called freedom of speech! Glorious freedom of speech! Go ahead and try to get an injunction against me. Try to stop the presses. You will only be telling the world who you are, and of that you should be ashamed. Besides, truth is a special category of free speech, because truth is speech protected.

The "Unknown Attorney" is now signing off. Until next time. . .Good luck and Good night! May the Lord be with you.

EVERYTHING YOU NEVER WANTED TO KNOW
ABOUT YOUR NONPROFIT CORPORATION

Watch for additional books by the Unknown Attorney coming to your bookstore soon!